Timeless Top 10 Travel Guides

PRAGUE

Top 10 Districts, Shopping and Dining, Museums, Activities, Historical Sights, Nightlife, Top Things to do Off the Beaten Path, and Much More!

By Tess Downey

Copyrights and Trademarks

All rights reserved. No part of this book may be reproduced or transformed in any form or by any means, graphic, electronic, or mechanical, including photocopying, recording, taping, or by any information storage retrieval system, without the written permission of the author.

This publication is Copyright ©2017. Nevada. All products, graphics, publications, software and services mentioned and recommended in this publication are protected by trademarks. In such instance, all trademarks & copyright belong to the respective owners. For information consult www.NRBpublishing.com

Disclaimer and Legal Notice

This product is not legal, medical, or accounting advice and should not be interpreted in that manner. You need to do your own due-diligence to determine if the content of this product is right for you. While every attempt has been made to verify the information shared in this publication, neither the author, neither publisher, nor the affiliates assume any responsibility for errors, omissions or contrary interpretation of the subject matter herein. Any perceived slights to any specific person(s) or organization(s) are purely unintentional.

We have no control over the nature, content and availability of the web sites listed in this book. The inclusion of any web site links does not necessarily imply a recommendation or endorse the views expressed within them. We take no responsibility for, and will not be liable for, the websites being temporarily unavailable or being removed from the internet.

The accuracy and completeness of information provided herein and opinions stated herein are not guaranteed or warranted to produce any particular results, and the advice and strategies, contained herein may not be suitable for every individual. Neither the author nor the publisher shall be liable for any loss incurred as a consequence of the use and application, directly or indirectly, of any information presented in this work. This publication is designed to provide information in regard to the subject matter covered. Neither the author nor the publisher assume any responsibility for any errors or omissions, nor do they represent or warrant that the ideas, information, actions, plans, suggestions contained in this book is in all cases accurate. It is the reader's responsibility to find advice before putting anything written in this book into practice. The information in this book is not intended to serve as legal, medical, or accounting advice.

Foreword

Prague, the Capital of the Czech Republic, is one of Europe's best and most preserved cities. Also known as the "Golden City of a Hundred Spires," Prague boasts striking façades, vibrant culture, rich history, and patriotic people. It's a very accessible city with many places to discover, many stories to hear, and plenty to experience.

In this book, you will learn everything you need to know about this wonderful and peaceful city. You will be provided with the top ten list of the best neighborhoods to stay in, best district to eat and chill, top destinations to visit, historically religious landmarks to know, hot spots at night, and many uncharted territories to explore. You will also be provided with all the essential things you need to know before travelling to this great city including the travel requirements, the do's and don'ts, the transportation system and the likes so that you can get in and around the city efficiently. Taste the wonderful culture that Prague and the Czech Republic have to offer and embark on a wonderful journey and find out why Prague is Europe's Golden City!

Table of Contents

Introduction 1

Chapter One: Prague Overview 5

    Prague in Focus 6

    A Brief History of Prague 8

    Prague's Language, People and Culture 13

Chapter Two: Travel Essentials 17

    Visa and Passport Requirements 18

    Seasons in Prague 32

Chapter Three: Getting In and Around Prague 37

Chapter Four: Hotels and Accommodations 49

    1. Prague 1 – The Old Town, The New Town, The Little Town, and Castle Town 51

    2. Prague 2 54

    3. Prague 3 56

    4. Prague 4 58

    5. Prague 5 60

    6. Prague 6 62

7. Prague 7 64

8. Prague 8 66

9. Prague 9 68

10. Prague 10 70

Chapter Five: Dining in Prague 73

1. Aromi 74

2. Bellevue 76

3. Blatouch 78

4. Café Imperial 79

5. Café Savoy 81

6. Cukrkvalimonda 83

7. Hergetova - Cihelna 85

8. Jahma 87

9. Klub - Architekt 88

10. U-Modr-Kachniky 90

Chapter Six: Tourist Destinations in Prague 93

1. Charles Bridge 94

2. Old Town Square 96

3. Prague Castle 98

4. Dancing House 100

5. Estates Theater 102

6. The Powder Gate 104

7. Municipal House 106

8. The Astronomical Clock and Old Town Hall Tower .. 108

9. Wenceslas Square 110

10. Vltava River 112

Chapter Seven: Religious Places in Prague 115

1. Tyn Church 116

2. St. Vitus Cathedral (Katedrála svatého Víta) 118

3. St. Nicholas Church of Old Town Square 120

4. Strahov Monastery (Strahovské nádvoří) 122

5. St. Peter and Paul Church 124

6. St. George's Basilica at Prague Castle (Bazilika Sv. Jiří) 126

7. Spanish Synagogue 128

8. Old New Synagogue 130

9. The Church of Our Lady Victorious..................................132

10. St. Salvator Church...133

Chapter Eight: Museums in Prague.......................................135

1. National Museum (Narodni Muzeum).........................136

2. Villa Amerika Dvorak Museum....................................137

3. St. Vitus Cathedral Museum...139

4. Lobkowicz Palace and Museum...................................140

5. Charles Bridge Museum..142

6. The Museum of Communism......................................144

7. Irish Museum of Modern Art.......................................146

8. DOX Centre for Contemporary Arts...........................147

9. Old Sewage Works Eco – Technical Museum............148

10. Mucha Museum...149

Chapter Nine: Nightlife in Prague...151

1. Club Sasazu...152

2. The Retro Club...154

3. Karlovy Lázně...156

4. Lucerna..158

5. Duplex 160

6. Radost FX 162

7. Estate House 164

8. The Meet Factory 166

9. Reduta Jazz Club 168

10. Bar and Books 170

Chapter Ten: Off - Beaten Path in Prague 173

1. Kolbenka Flea Market 174

2. Holesovice Neighborhood 175

3. Naplavka River Walk 177

4. Jewish Cemeteries 178

5. Zizkov 179

6. The Nový Svět 181

7. Sea World 182

8. Mirror Maze 183

9. Golden Lane 185

10. Olomouc 186

Quick Travel Guide 189

Prague Highlights 190

1. Prague Quick Facts 190

2. Transportation 191

3. Travel Essentials 192

Prague Highlights 195

PHOTO REFERENCES 201

REFERENCES 211

Introduction

Prague is a city filled with exuberant landmarks, and sumptuous Art Nouveau. Its streets are filled with amazing music, friendly people, vivacious architecture, and of course, colorful pubs that serves up some of the best drinks Europe has to offer! Although Prague is not something that people easily had on their mind when it comes to visiting European cities, the capital is still thriving with tourists around the world.

Introduction

Czechkoslovakia was divided into two states – the Czech Republic, and Slovakia. And in 1993, the Czech Republic officially gained its independence. One of the most preserved medieval cities at the heart of Europe lies the former capital of Czechkoslovakia which is Prague. Prague as well as some parts of Czechkoslovakia was once under the rule of a historical entity or kingdom around the Middle Ages called Bohemia, which is why the city's heritage and culture originated from the Bohemians. Prague was also the only city in Central Europe to practice democracy for many decades.

Once you get to this place the first thing you will notice is how the whole city is laid out just like during medieval times – it's cobblestone streets, its flea markets, the city's various grand architectures from castles to cathedrals, and its building's eclectic designs altogether will make you feel as if Prague was still stuck at the time of kings and kingdoms!

The city's skylines are filled with the towers of various historical churches and castles that dates back thousands of years ago which is why the city earned its name as the "Golden City of a Hundred Spires." It's towering basilicas and castles with magnificent Middle Ages architecture like Baroque, Gothic, andRomanesque will

Introduction

surely bring you back to one of the most historical time in human history.

Today, the city is becoming a modern metropolis. Entrepreneurs and artists continue to thrive and expand in this country. There are now various local boutiques, and shops including international brands, dining places, hotels, and modern luxuries as well as efficient transportations that run the whole city. Its locals are now progressing to a much high – tech kind of living but their culture and preserved heritage way back from their Bohemian ancestors still lives on!

In this book, you will learn the basic things you need to know about Prague: its preserved location, its history, its people, its language, culture, traditions and way of living. You will also be given information regarding your travel needs, and of course overviews of the top tourist attractions, districts, and food places as well as hidden facets of the city to make sure you don't miss an authentic European experience.

Introduction

Chapter One: Prague Overview

Before you set foot in this golden city, it is essential to know specific details of what you're about to deal with. Prague has historically rich beginnings until it was officially divided into four main districts. The present day city is now being transformed into a modern and commercialize city – center. You might want to consider discovering facts about this place so that you know what to expect before you go about in your itinerary and to avoid getting into trouble.

In this chapter, you will be provided with an overview of Prague – its city, language, culture, people, and of course history!

Chapter One: Prague Overview

Prague in Focus

The Czech Republic is located on the center of Europe, and its capital dominant city is Prague. Prague is travelling near the Vltava River, and all its famous landmarks including the Old Town Square, Prague Castle, Charles Bridge, and Wenceslas Square is very easy on foot, it's all just about an hour's walk. The city is also the center for business and government affairs; it is home to the Czech's President as well as other governmental institutions and official organizations of the country.

There are about 1.2 million locals residing in its metropolitan area, and because of the city's continuous development and commercialization, more locals and foreigners choose to stay in the city for good.

During the 14th century, the Holy Roman Emperor ruled and led in this city. It was also Prague's golden age because at that time the commerce and cultural sector was flourishing. Back then, Prague was one of Europe's most highly cultured and largest cities. Around the 1800, the city was divided into four separate and fortified towns namely; The Castle Town – where Czech rulers and royal leaders reside for thousands of years; The Little Town – which is just behind the Castle Town, where nobles and aristocrats live to be close to the King; The Old Town, bolstering with its magnificent market square; and lastly The New Town where

Chapter One: Prague Overview

the grand Wenceslas Square is located, providing a stage for the Czech Republic's tumultuous 20th century history.

Prague's depressing decades of communist control for most residents only feels like a distant memory because the city is now bustling with entrepreneurial energy, excited tourists, and modern day way of living. Everything you see, like one of the famous buildings called The Dancing House which is also known as "Fred and Ginger," and the vibrant crowd of locals and tourists wandering around the streets seem to celebrate Czech's freedom.

The city is also a shopping paradise filled with diverse shops and unique boutiques. Walking around Prague's shopping alleys truly mesmerizes visitors; it also makes a picture perfect photo because of the building's architecture, old – century like ground, and colorful vibe. It's also a city flourishing with great lanes that will lead you to uncharted places, and has a plenty of vibrant markets. You'll feel the medieval vibe as you shop around for food and other fetishes.

Prague is also the mecca for musicians; in fact, Mozart loved that place so much that one of his famous pieces called "Dan Giovanni" debuted in the city. Another great classical musician Anton Dvorak lived and composed most of his famous songs in Prague as well including a symphony called From the New World, American String Quartet, and operas

Chapter One: Prague Overview

like Rusalka, Humoresque and Songs My Mother Taught Me.

The great thing is that Prague locals continue to carry that musical enthusiasm. You can find several box offices around town that offers a variety of music and recital performances including theater, opera, jazz, and classical. Tickets are very cheap which is why tourists like you shouldn't miss it for the world. What's more interesting is that you can choose from many great venues chamber music halls that abound the city.

A Brief History of Prague

Before Prague was known as the "Golden City of a Hundred Spires," and before it became the hub of tourists all over the world it had gone through different phases and major changes; let's take a look at its colorful past so we can appreciate the city's present and look forward to its future.

Middle Ages:

- 870: Slavs landed in the Czech Republic around 6th century, and they also built a castle in the city of Prague. Around the 10th century the city was thriving as merchants and local culture abound the area.

- 973: Prague was given a bishop as their leader.

Chapter One: Prague Overview

- 13th – 14th Century: During this time, Prague was the go – to place of German craftsmen as well as merchants, and by the 14th century it became one of Europe's most important cities.

- 1232: Friars or preachers came to Prague. Friars are like monks but they are more of a preachers going from one community to another.

- 1270: The Jewish community began forming around the city and The Old – New Synagogue was founded. Unfortunately, most of them are being persecuted.

- 1334: The Roman Emperor, Charles IV decided to live and rule in Prague. The appointed bishop now became an archbishop. This was the golden age of the city.

- 1344: They began building the St. Vitus's Cathedral

- 1348: The Holy Roman Emperor Charles IV established the Prague University, and rebuilt Prague's Castle.

- 1357: The Czech began to build the Charles Bridge in honor of their Holy Emperor

Chapter One: Prague Overview

- 1364: Prague Town Hall was built and founded.

- 1389: A record of about 3,000 Jews was killed in the city.

- 1415: Prague's Jan Hus who was a Christian Martyr in the Middle Ages died.

Renaissance Period:

- 1601: Tycho Brahe, one of the greatest Danish Astronomer died in Prague, and was buried in Tyn Church

- 1621: About 30 Protestant leaders were slaughtered in Old Town Square

- 1630: Wallenstein Palace was founded. And despite political and religious turmoil, the 17th century was a great time for Prague

- 1689: The Old Town was caught in fire and it was eventually rebuilt by the people.

- 1713: The city suffered a huge outbreak of plague

Chapter One: Prague Overview

- 1741 – 1742: France occupied and conquered Prague

- 1744: Prussians occupied the city, and yet had another siege around 1757.

- 1783: Estates Theater was established, and the city continues to flourish economically and culturally around the 18th century.

- 1784: Prague was officially divided into four united towns (The Castle Town The Little Town, The Old Town, and The New Town)

19th Century Prague

- 1818: The National Museum was established, many buildings were built, and it is around this time that Czech nationalism flourished and grew rapidly

- 1845: Start of the Industrial Revolution; this is also the time where the railway system was first established in the city
- 1885: The Museum of Decorative Arts was established

- 1891: The famous Petrin View Tower was erected

Chapter One: Prague Overview

20th Century

- 1915: The people built a monument for Jan Hus, the Christian Martyr of the middle ages.

- 1918: Prague officially became the capital of Czechoslovakia, and around this time the city's growth was steady and continuous. Around 1939, the city hit a 1 million population.

- 1939: The Nazis during the World War conquered Prague. Fortunately, most of the buildings weren't completely destroyed, only a little bit damaged but Jewish residents living in the area were killed.

- 1945: The people began a rebellion against the Germans, and by May 8th of the same year, Germany withdrew from Prague.

- 1948: Czechoslovakia's communists once again seized the city, and the era of repression began.

- 1968: Alexander Dubcek started a reform called the Prague Spring but it was put to an end by the August Warsaw Pact forces when they invaded the country, however, the communist party collapsed in 1989.

Chapter One: Prague Overview

21st Century

- 1993: The Czech Republic became an independent state with Prague as its capital.

- 2002 - Present: Prague was devastated by flooding in 2002 but the city recovered. Prague continues to flourish and thrive thanks to the modernization and commercialization. The city has now 1.2 million residents.

Prague's Language, People and Culture

Chapter One: Prague Overview

The official language of the city and the Czech Republic is Czech. Locals can also understand simple Slavic languages including Croatian, Polish, Serbian and Bosnian. The Slovak language is also commonly understood by locals since Czech and Slovak natives have historically communicated with each other for many years. Both languages are quite similar and can be mutually understood without the need of a translator.

Young people also know how to speak and understand the English language. If in case you'll go to boutiques, restaurants, places, airports or bars among many, you'll be able to understand the directions, menus, signage's etc. Police officers, personnel, and maybe some middle age people may not speak English very well.

You can also try and speak Russian since some people who went to school before the Velvet Revolution studied the language (mostly around 30 - 40 year olds might have some knowledge). Be polite though because some people may dislike Russians as well as communists due to occupying Czechoslovakia back in 1968. Some Czechs also know how to speak German, but of course learning a little bit of their own language will make you connected to the locals you interact with.

If you want to really experience the culture and the people, you should try joining a native or local city tour, not only will you get to enjoy the city like a local; you'll also be

Chapter One: Prague Overview

with the real locals. You can join small groups around town conducting such tours; it's usually a 90 minute walking tour where the natives share their love and passion for this vibrant city. The best part is that, this walking tour service is absolutely free! Tipping is of course optional. You can learn more about the landmarks, and everyday life of people through the eyes of a local. These educational and fun guided tours are surely worth taking!

Aside from exploring the city and joining various local tours around, you can also have fun experiencing different activities like biking, photography tours, escape room games, sightseeing river cruises, theatrical and musical performances, and if you're right on time, you can also witness how they celebrate their festivals. You'll never run out of activities to do and places to explore in this peaceful city.

Chapter One: Prague Overview

Chapter Two: Travel Essentials

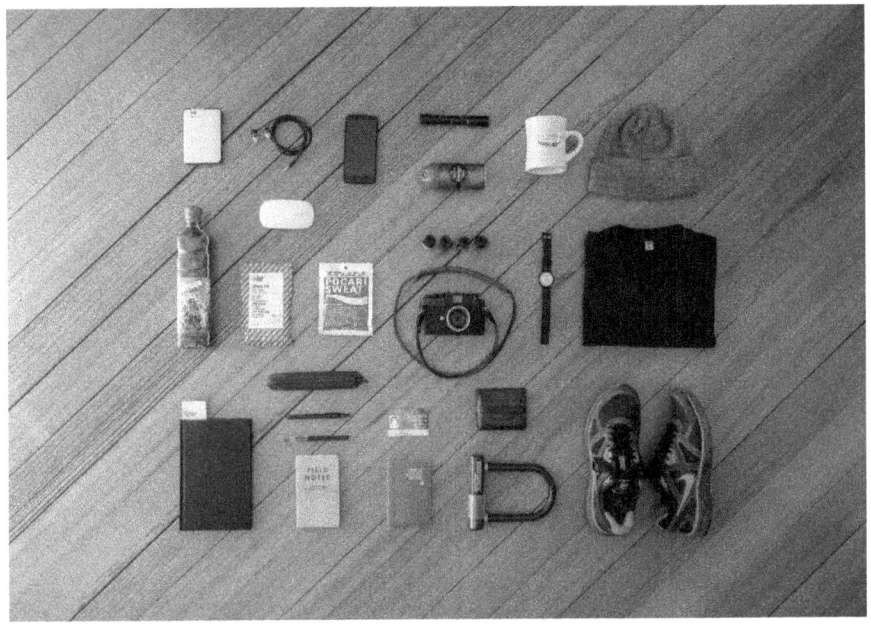

Now that you have learned several things about Prague, and already have general knowledge of the city, the next thing for you to learn about and accomplish before actually going there is the travelling requirements or traveller's info. The travel requirements and some basic reminders in planning your trip to this city are essential in order for you to have a wonderful experience and not get into trouble especially in immigration and customs. In this chapter, you will learn what you need to do for you to be able to travel to Prague, Czech Republic.

Chapter Two: Travel Essentials

You will learn the things you need to bring and be aware of as well as essential information for first time travellers such as money, and communication.

Visa and Passport Requirements

The Czech Republic is part of the European Union (EU) as well as the Schengen area which means that tourists from countries that are also a member of the EU is not required to have a visa, just a valid ID and passport. Generally speaking, if you are a tourist, you need to have a passport with 6 months of validity from your departure date and you are only allowed to stay in the country for 90 days or 3 months.

Chapter Two: Travel Essentials

For citizens of nations that is included in the European Economic Area (EEA) you are also not required to have a visa to enter the country or those visitors who already have a Schengen visa. If you are going directly to Prague or through another Schengen country, you don't need to worry about visa requirements.

If you are also a family member of an EU citizen, even if you are not a permanent resident or only hold a temporary permit from other EU countries, you're not required to acquire a visa.

However, if you are planning to stay longer in Prague or the Czech Republic for an extended vacation or other private matters, you may need to show proof that you have sufficient funds that will last you for your intended period. You may also be asked to show a confirmed onward and return flight tickets, and also the address of the place you're going to stay in/ hotel booking confirmation.

Aside from the countries mentioned above, here are the lists of nations that are also allowed in Czech Republic without a visa, same rules apply but there may also be some restrictions for selected countries.

Chapter Two: Travel Essentials

- Albania
- Andorra
- Antigua and Bermuda
- Argentina
- Australia
- Bahamas
- Barbados
- Bosnia and Herzegovina
- Brazil
- Brunei
- Canada
- Chile
- Costa Rica
- Croatia
- Guatemala
- Honduras
- Hong Kong
- Israel
- Japan
- Macedonia
- Macao
- Malaysia
- Mauritius
- Mexico
- Monaco
- Montenegro
- New Zealand
- Nicaragua
- Panama
- Paraguay
- Saint Christopher & Nevis
- Salvador
- San Marino
- Serbia
- Seychelles
- Singapore
- South Korea
- Taiwan
- Trinidad and Tobago
- Uruguay
- USA
- Vatican
- Venezuela

Chapter Two: Travel Essentials

For citizens of nations that are not included in the list mentioned above, you are required to acquire a Schengen Visa to enter Czech Republic or even other countries that are part of the European Union. For more information, we recommend visiting Czech Republic's Official Immigration Website or visit any Czech embassy in your home country if any.

You cannot find a visa application office at the Prague Airport or any border crossings; if you arrived without a Schengen visa you won't be granted access to the country.

Tourists and visitors should pass the Immigration and Security Checkpoints in various points of entry. Tourists are also not allowed to engage in any form of occupation, profession, business or any form of paid employment while in the country. You also maybe ask to register your visa with the police within 3 days upon your arrival.

Traveller's Info

In this section, you will be provided with essential traveler's information on what to do and what not to do in Prague. Be sure to keep all these essentials in mind while you are traveling.

Chapter Two: Travel Essentials

Money Exchange, ATMs, and Credit Cards

Czech Republic's currency is called Czech Crown (or koruna). The local abbreviation of the currency is Kč, while the international abbreviation is CZK. If you want to know the current official exchange rate, please visit the website of the Czech National Bank.

Exchange counters and offices abound in Prague especially in major tourist attractions, however these offices offer very bad rates plus they also charge other fees. You should also ask employee/s first on how much you would get if you exchange a certain amount before giving them your money so you can compare rates with other offices if ever.

It's highly recommended that you exchange your money at eXchange office that you can find in the city – center. Its office is located at 115 Kaprova Street, 14/13 Prague. You can print out a VIP coupon form online for you to get a good VIP rates. Their office is open until 8 PM only. You can also go to the Main Railway Station in Hlavní nádraží because there are many exchange centers there that offer good rates as well as the Alfa Prague located in the Palladium's Shopping Center.

ATMs can be found in major parts of the city such as airports, hotels, shopping centers and in main banks. It is

Chapter Two: Travel Essentials

available 24/7. However, ATMs in Prague charges huge extra fees, and also give you a bad exchange rate. It's recommended to withdraw from Unicredit Bank ATM because it'll give you the right exchange rate and may not charge you high fees.

Credit cards such as Visa, MasterCard and American Express may be accepted in various hotels, restaurants, car rentals and shops but it is selected only. However, it may not come in handy if you are staying in a remote area such as villages and small towns, or areas that are away from tourist spots. It's better to bring cash than rely on your credit or debit card to be sure. It's also possible to pay with Euros or British Pounds in various fast food chains and international stores.

It's also highly advice that you don't exchange money on the streets because there are various gang operations near exchange centers that are targeting tourists. Never ever accept any offers of monetary exchanges on the streets or from unknown people.

Electricity and Voltage

Prague's standard electrical voltage is 220 – 240 volts AC (50 cycles). Majority of the plugs and electric outlets are European standard electrical sockets called the Type C

Europlug as well as Type E, and Type F Schuko. You may need a transformer or converter to aid your electrical equipment or appliances. It is highly recommended that you buy the three common kinds of adaptors to make sure that you can charge while in Prague.

You may also buy electrical adaptors or transformers from various convenience and electrical/gadget stores in your own country so you can easily specify the equipment you need. You may need to use a plug adapter and step – down transformer for European appliances that requires 110 – 120 Volts.

Public Holidays

Just like any other cities and countries, Prague also observes lots of different public holidays and religious festivities. Take note of the following dates and events so you can plan your trip accordingly.

- **January 1st** – Restoration Day of the Independent Czech State, New Year's Day
- **Good Friday**
- **Easter Monday**
- **May 1st** – Labour Day
- **May 8th** – Liberation Day
- **July 5th** – Saints Cyril and Methodius Day

- **July 6th** - Jan Hus Day
- **September 28th** - St. Wenceslas Day (Czech Statehood Day)
- **October 28th** - Independent Czechoslovak State Day
- **November 17th** - Struggle for Freedom and Democracy Day
- **December 24th** - Christmas Eve
- **December 25th** - Christmas Day
- **December 26th** - St. Stephen's Day

Health and Safety

You don't necessarily need vaccination certificates or other medical certificates upon entering the Czech Republic, although it's better to check if your airline requires it. If you happen to bring to your pets, you need to show its health or medical clearances to ensure that they have been vaccinated and free of rabies. You need to check with your airlines if they will allow it on – board. Please also check the consular website regarding the breed or the type of animal you can bring to Prague.

- **Potable Water**

Tap water in Prague is clean and approved by the World Health Organization which is therefore safe to drink. It is free for locals and tourists. Mineral waters, including imported brands, can be found in stores and restaurants as well as airports or transportation terminals, although most tourists opt to buy bottled waters.

- **Hospitals**

Hospitals in Prague are of a very high quality; you don't have to worry, if in case you had a medical emergency or accidents because the city has very large hospitals and medical staff that attends to foreign visitors. Both public and private hospitals offer the highest quality of medical care and hospital facilities. The medical fee for attendance depends on the hospital and the procedure that will be done; patients will always be treated even if they cannot pay immediately, although the regulations may vary. Most medical professionals in public and private sectors can speak in English.

The three most recommended hospitals are:
- Na Homolce Hospital
- Polyclinic at Narodni
- Canadian Medical Care

Chapter Two: Travel Essentials

- **Smoking Restrictions**

Smoking is prohibited in various public areas in Prague such as bus and tram stops, metro stations, healthcare facilities, and cultural buildings. As of May 31 2017, smoking in all dining places or restaurants (except the smoking area) is also prohibited.

You may pay a penalty or be put to jail if you will not observe the law. There is a designated floor in various hotels where you can smoke. Obviously, you are not allowed to smoke in air-conditioned areas or facilities.

Customs

Upon arriving at the airport in Prague, you will need to be cleared by the department of customs or Immigration Officers. Here are the things you are allowed to bring to and from Czech Republic:

Things You Can Bring to the Czech Republic:

Custom checks are pretty easy in Czech Republic, you can come through without opening your baggage, they aren't that strict but of course, there are still some guidelines that you need to follow.

Chapter Two: Travel Essentials

International visitors can bring most personal items including the following special items:

- 200 cigarettes, 50 cigars, 250 grams of tobacco
- 1 liter of spirits over 22% volume, 2 liters of fortified wine or sparkling wine, or 2 liters of still wine
- 50 grams of perfume
- 250ml of eau de toilette

Restricted Items
- Meat/meat products
- Milk and dairy products
- Plants and wildlife
- Illegal narcotics (including marijuana and other drugs/ drug paraphernalia)
- Weapons like guns, and explosives (unless you are legit to carry one)
- Pornographic materials

The are no limits on the amount of money you can bring, however, you must declare it (if it exceeds 10,000 €) to the Czech Republic Customs office to prove that it is the same amount you have before entering the country, therefore you can also take out the same amount or less once you depart.

Chapter Two: Travel Essentials

For more information on what you can take home from the country please contact the following agencies for the following nationality:

U.S. Citizens:
Tel. Number: (877) 287-8667
Website: www.cbp.gov

Canadian Citizens:
Tel. Number: (800) 461-9999/ (204) 983-3500
Website: www.cbsa-asfc.gc.ca

Australian Citizens:
Tel. Number: (1300) 363-263
Website: www.customs.gov.au

New Zealand Citizens:
Tel. Number: (04) 473-6099
Website: www.customs.govt.nz

Travel and Medical Insurances

It is highly recommended that you acquire travel insurance before traveling to Prague. Inquire with your travel insurance company about the emergency coverage, contact numbers, and persons as well as the insurance policy. If you already have one, always carry with you the insurance policy and the insurance company hotline number for identification purposes in cases of emergencies.

Chapter Two: Travel Essentials

For citizens of EU countries, you are entitled to receive a free emergency treatment as long as you have your European Health Insurance Card (EHIC); it's available in health centers in your home country. If you are a citizen of non – EU countries, you need to pay in cash but you can apply for reimbursement from your insurance providers. Just make sure to keep all the documents or receipts from the hospital you have been admitted to.

Communication Services

Another central necessity that you need to have access to is the transmission lines and services. Obviously, when you get to another country, the mobile services, as well as internet services, will be different. Here are some things you need to keep in mind for you to be able to communicate effectively while you are in Prague.

- **Mobile Phones/Telephones**

Telephone booths still exist in the city but they are only a few and may not be accessible. Most phones require a prepaid calling card that you can purchase from magazine kiosks or tobacco booths. They cost around 200Kc to 500Kc. The telephone country code of Czech Republic is 420. You have to dial first the international access code of the country you're going to call, then add 420 plus the phone number.

Chapter Two: Travel Essentials

For direct calls just dial 00, the country code, the area code and the telephone number you're calling.

Cell phone rentals are not that widespread in the city – center, so you will most likely rely on your phone while you are in the city to make local or international calls easily. You can choose to buy a pay – as – you – go SIM card plus a prepaid calling card in town. You may also opt to open your roaming services, although the charges will be a bit expensive (overseas charges) if you send international SMS or calls. UK cellphones may work without any problem as long as you activate international roaming features.

- **Wi-Fi/ Internet Services**

The Wi-Fi and internet services in Prague are not that accessible. If you will be staying at hotels, they may also charge you for it, and the signal may drop if you're far from their routers. Don't expect any internet connections in remote areas. Even if there aren't many hotspots around the city, a god connection may still be available in primary public locations and tourist destinations such as department stores, centers, restaurants and dining places, hotels that are free of use but some may require you to purchase something.

Internet cafes, some hotels, and business centers also offering internet access but you may need to pay for it to rent the computers. The average internet rate is 1 – 2 Kc per minute of surfing. Just ask your hotel on where you can find the nearest internet cafes.

Emergency Numbers

You may need to keep these emergency numbers on your phone just in case any issues arise while you are in Prague:

- **General Emergency Number** – dial 112 on the telephone
- **National Police** – dial 158 on the telephone
- **Ambulance/ER Rescue** – dial 155 on the telephone
- **Fire Department** – dial 150 on the telephone
- **Metropolitan Police** - dial 158 on the telephone

Seasons in Prague

Prague has 4 seasons like most European cities; spring begins from March to May, summer starts from June until August, September to October is autumn season, while winter begins around November to the month of February. There's a perfect balance between sunny and cold climate in this city, and it's usually great to have a tour all year round.

Chapter Two: Travel Essentials

In this section, you will learn what to expect in Prague's climate and weather so you can plan your trip accordingly.

Best Time to Visit Prague: Spring

According to locals and tourists, spring is the best time to visit Prague. As mentioned earlier, spring starts from March until May. This is a great time for tourists to explore this vibrant city because the weather is not too hot or too cold plus places aren't packed with tourists unlike during summer time. Perfect for those who love to explore the city without too much hustles and bustles.

The temperature ranges around 40 – 60 degrees Celsius, but it's better to also prepare because even if the days are longer and warmer, the winds could still be quite breezy and cool so make sure you wear jackets/coats. Aside from that you can also attend several events between these months. Events like the Prague Marathon, Prague Food Fest, Prague Int'l Music Fest, and the Czech Beer Festival all happens from May to June.

Summer in Prague

Summer starts from June to August. You can expect a very dry and sunny climate that can go as high as 70 degrees Celsius. Summer in Prague is the time where most tourists from all over the world and from neighboring European countries arrived. Expect crowds of visitors everywhere from cafes, dining places to tourist attractions and hotels. It's highly recommended that you book in advance (at least 2 weeks before your date of arrival) so that you can have better options and also be able to make reservations. Many people flock during the summer because it has a great atmosphere, and also perfect for sightseeing.

Summer time in Prague also means a cheaper price for various tours and activities since many tourists visit the city but hotel, accommodations and restaurants can be quite expensive since it is a peak season, be sure to bring extra pocket money. If you can't handle the crowd of tourists, summer is not the best time for you to visit, but if you're in for a hot summer and love to hang out with fellow visitors, then book a trip around these month. Key events include Prague Proms, Venetian Nights, United Islands, and Kafka's Death Anniversary.

<u>Autumn Season</u>

Another great time to visit Prague is from September to October, its major advantage is that there aren't many tourists compared to previous months, and the weather is also good. Temperature ranges from 40 – 60 degrees Celsius so be sure to wear a couple of layers. The events you can witness include Dvorak's Prague Fest, and the Birell Prague Grand Prix.

Chapter Two: Travel Essentials

Winter Season

If you want to challenge yourself while exploring this preserved city, then winter time is suited for you. You can expect almost no tourists at all! You can pretty much enjoy the city, feel it has a cool breeze, and also get cheaper accommodations. Make sure to wear layers of clothes because the temperature can drop to 20 degrees and has an average high of about 30 degrees Celsius.

Key events you can attend are the Prague Christmas Market, Int'l Festival of Wind Orchestras, Prague Winter Festival and the Bohemian Carnival. It's a great time to celebrate Christmas with your family in Prague!

Some Travel Tips

- Do not eat or drink in public transportations.

- Do not leave your valuables unattended. Your money, passport or travel documents should be in a safe place, or you should carry it with you at all times.

- Maintain cleanliness and clean as you go.

- Always bring a bottled water to avoid dehydration during summer.

Chapter Two: Travel Essentials

- Be vigilant and watch out for your valuables especially in crowded places.

- Beware of thieves, the most common threat in Prague is petty crimes such as pickpockets, gang operations on the streets, and other scams.

- Never easily hand over your IDs or important documents if some random police officer or stranger ask but will never ask for any cash or your credit card.

- Observe the rules and regulations of public places especially inside shopping malls and tourist spots

- Don't litter, drink and drive or urinate in public venues, for you not to get caught or fined by authorities or worse get arrested.

- Always bring an umbrella and jacket especially during winter or rainy seasons.

Chapter Three: Getting In and Around Prague

After learning the different requirements you need before traveling to this beautiful city, the next thing you should know is how to navigate around it. Prague is quite a small place and various landmarks are walking distance. Its cobbled streets are perfectly set up for foreign tourists and adventurous locals. If you have enough knowledge regarding Prague's port of entry and transportation services, you will quickly get to your destination with ease. Learning how to navigate Prague is the key so that you can have an amazing experience visiting one of Europe's most preserved cities.

Chapter Three: Getting In and Around In Prague

In this chapter, you will learn the major transportation systems and port of entries as well as its corresponding estimated fares. You'll also learn how the city's communication services can help you stay connected. Travelling tips are also provided.

Travelling to Prague by Plane

If you're coming in from a different country or outside of Europe, it's best to travel by plane. The Prague Airport is the city's international gateway to the Czech Republic.

It is located in Ruzyne which is about 12 miles or 18 km northwest of the center. You can either land in terminals North 1 and North 2. The North 1 terminal handles overseas flights to and from European countries, United Kingdom, and also United States; on the other hand, North 2 handles so – called internal flights to and from countries like Germany, Italy, France, Switzerland, and other countries in Europe.

Czech's international carrier is the Czech Airline that operates directly to and from the JFK airport in New York, Atlanta as well as Toronto, Canada. Other international and European airlines including Delta Airlines also offer direct service to and from the city.

Chapter Three: Getting In and Around In Prague

Once you arrived at the airport, you can either take the Taxi to get you into the city (but they are quite expensive) or you can get into a more reliable yellow cab called AAA RadioTaxi.

The average rate is around 600 Kc, and it usually takes about half an hour from the airport to the city proper but can go longer if it's a rush hour. If you're looking for a cheaper way to get into the city from the airport, you can choose to ride CEDAZ minibuses as well as other public transportations like city buses or Airport Express buses.

Travelling to Prague by Car

If you are coming from neighboring European cities or within the Czech Republic, Prague can be accessed through Europe's major highway including the D1 Motorway (with connections in Brno, Bratislava, Krakow, and Budapest), D5 Motorway 9with connections to Plzen, Nuremberg, Italy and western/southern Europe), and the D8 Motorway (with connections from Dresden and Berlin).

You can also get rental cars from various international agencies. However, you should be 18 years old and above (some require 23 or 25 yrs. old), and has a driver's license from your own country. This option can be convenient but it is also costly; the average rental is 750Kc a day/unlimited

Chapter Three: Getting In and Around In Prague

mileage for economy cars to 1,500Kc per day for a full-sized or huge cars.

You can rent in advance online, rent from in – town agencies or get services from local agencies rather than the airport (because airport surcharges applies) so that you can get a lower rate.

Travelling to Prague by Train

You can also travel to the city by riding European rail lines with various connections from different cities like Berlin, Brno, Vienna, Dresden, Bratislava as well as Budapest. If you're coming from Vienna, you can also ride the Pendolino rail service that has high – speed direct service to Prague cutting travelling time to as short as 4 hours. Prague's main international train station is called Hlavní nádrazí with passengers coming to and from Vienna, Budapest and Berlin. You can find more information by calling 840-112-113 or visiting their website at <http://jizdnirady.idnes.cz>

Travelling to Prague by Bus

Prague's central bus station in Florenc, Krizíkova is also near the main train station. Local and long – distance buses arrives in the central bus station. Florenc station is

Chapter Three: Getting In and Around In Prague

quite small, you can also find smaller bus stations at Zelivského (metro line A), Smíchovské nádrazí (metro line B), and Nádrazí Holesovice (metro line C).

Getting Around Prague on Foot

The city of Prague has cobbled and paved flooring and has plenty of lanes that can lead you to magnificent views. The distance of one landmark to another is only a few minute walk, and although places are relatively close, you should still wear comfortable shoes so you can enjoy your walk around the city.

If you are looking for a certain address or neighborhood, don't worry because you can easily find them. Besides, getting lost in this vibrant city can be a great thing because it will give you a chance to get to know the city better.

Here are some of the districts and corresponding neighborhood in Prague:

District 1:
- Hradcany
- Malá Strana
- Staré Mesto
- Josefov

Chapter Three: Getting In and Around In Prague

- Northern Nové Mesto

District 2:

- Southern Nové Mesto
- Vysehrad
- Western Vinohrady

District 3:

- Eastern Vinohrady
- Zizkov

District 4:

- Western Bubenec
- Dejvice
- Vokovice
- Stresovice
- Brevnov
- Veleslavín
- Liboc
- Ruzyne
- Repy
- Nebusice
- Lysolaje

Chapter Three: Getting In and Around In Prague

- Sedlec
- Suchdol

District 5:

- Holesovice
- Letná

Getting Around by Trams and Buses

Prague's public transportation is consists of network of trams and buses. These vehicles offer a cheaper way of getting around the city while enjoying the sights with the locals and fellow tourists. There are about 24 tram lines that abound the city. The Tram No. 22 is often called the Tourist Tram but be careful because locals also call it the Pickpocket Express, it usually runs to top tourist attractions like the Prague Castle and the National Theater. Tram services are reduced after midnight (usually a one – hour interval). Buses also run until midnight in selected routes, and they mostly go to routes of Prague's older districts. Both tramlines and buses have its own stops and stations, and it both starts operating at 4:30 AM.

Chapter Three: Getting In and Around In Prague

Fares for Trams and Buses:

- **Single – Journey Tickets** (good for 5 stations): 18Kc or 9Kc for 6 years old to 15 year old (children below 6 year old are free).
- **Unlimited Ticket (for trams, metro trains, buses) Single – Journey Tickets:** 26Kc for adults (16 year old and above)
- **1 – Day Pass for Unlimited Travel:** 100Kc
- **3 – Day Pass for Unlimited Travel:** 330Kc
- **5 – Day Pass for Unlimited Travel:** 500Kc

Where to Buy:

You can buy from coin – operated machines (yellow in color) located in metro stations and newsstands with the Trafika signage. Make sure to validate your ticket in the stamping machine before hopping on any trams or buses, and don't throw it away for the duration of your ride because ticket collectors may check it. If you lose your ticket or have an invalid ticket, you will be asked to pay a fine of 700Kc - 950Kc.

Chapter Three: Getting In and Around In Prague

Getting Around by Metro Trains

If you want to make the most of your trip in this beautiful city, you should take advantage of its train system, as with any other big cities, the public transportation is the best way to get in and around the area. Metro Train System abounds in Prague, what's great is that the tickets are cheap, the service is great, and the travelling is very efficient. As a matter of fact, most locals don't own vehicles and don't even bother on how to drive because of its effective train system.

Prague's metro lines operate daily from 5am to midnight and have a 2 to 10 minute interval. There are 3 lines of metro trains that can be identified by color and letter: A (green), B (yellow), and C (red).

Common Route/Stations:

- Muzeum (Line A and C)
- Mustek (Line A and B)
- Malostranská (Line A)

Getting Around by Funicular

Funicular is a cog railway in Prague that takes tourists up and down the famous Petrin Hill. You can ride this scenic route daily from 9am to 11:30pm with 10 – 15 minutes interval. What's great is that it also makes a stop

Chapter Three: Getting In and Around In Prague

halfway up the hill in Nebozízek restaurant that has a spectacular view of the city. The ticket price is 26Kc.

Getting Around by Taxi

Exploring the city by taxi may not be ideal because there has been many reports of tourists getting ripped off by taxi drivers (especially if you hail them in tourist spots, main train stations, and/or fancy hotels), although the system has now improved.

If you still want to travel via taxi, it's highly recommended that you just call the cab company directly. You can choose from AAA Radiotaxi company (tel. 14014 or 222-333-222), ProfiTaxi (tel. 844-700-800), or SEDOP (tel. 841-666-333) so that you can find honest and reliable cab drivers.

The average cost around the city is 100Kc to 200Kc depending on how far or near your destination is from the point of pick-up. If you hail a taxi from the city - center to the airport, it will cost you around 600Kc.

Fares:

- Reliable meter starts at 40Kc if you hail a cab on the street
- If you hail a cab by phone: 30Kc
- Per kilometer rate: 28Kc

Chapter Three: Getting In and Around In Prague

Tips when Riding Taxis:

- Never get into an unmarked cab
- You should ask the driver on entering what the approximate fare will be to your destination. He may not know exactly, but he should be able to give you an estimate
- Make sure the driver has switched on the meter, otherwise get off the cab
- Tell the driver you will need a receipt at the end of the ride

Getting Around by Car

Driving around town is not recommended because the streets are usually filled with people, and one – way streets make it hard to reach certain places, not to mention the parking centers are usually restricted for tourists, and are only available for residents with parking stickers. However, if you are planning to explore other cities of the Czech Republic then it's probably better to drive a car.

If you want a cheaper or affordable price, you can negotiate to get the best possible deal and also avail discounts. Usually, car rental companies offer various deal or special options like keeping the car for an extended period with unlimited mileage, or renting a bigger car for a

Chapter Three: Getting In and Around In Prague

relatively cheaper cost. Don't forget to bring your driver's license, and other necessary IDs or documents needed.

Here's a list of the International Car Rental Companies in Prague:

- Try Europcar: Tel. 224-811-290; www.europcar.cz
- Hertz (Tel. 225-345-031; www.hertz.cz)
- Budget (Tel. 220-560-443; www.budget.cz)

Here's a list of the Local Car Rental Companies in Prague:

- Czechocar (Tel. 261-222-079 or 261-222-143; www.czechocar.cz)
- SeccoCar (Tel. 220-800-647; www.seccocar.cz)

Getting Around by Bike

If you wanted to explore the city by yourself and get fit at the same time, you can ride around with bicycles. The good thing is that the city built bike lanes that run from Vltava River as well as the Prague Zoo. Mountain bikes or bicycles with thick tires are ideal since the city is mostly made up of cobblestone roads.

You can rent bikes and also join bike tours by signing up with companies like Praha Bike (Tel. 732-388-880; www.prahabike.cz), and City Bike (Tel. +420 776 180 284; www.citybike-prague.com).

Chapter Four: Hotels and Accommodations

After learning about the ports of entry in Prague and the different ways on how you can get around this very historical city, the next thing you should know after arriving at the airport is where to stay. There are tons of options online and a lot of feedback from friends, and family who have stayed in the city - not to mention the thousands of social reviews and comments on different social networking sites. Choosing where to stay for the duration of your trip is very important because it can save you a lot of time when it comes to touring the city, and can also make your budget go a long way in terms of food, transportation services etc.

Chapter Four: Hotels and Accommodations

In this chapter you will be provided with the list of what we consider to be the top 10 best hotel and accommodation districts in Prague. Some are very expensive, while others are a bit more cost-friendly.

You will also be given an overview of what to expect in a particular district, and the landmarks or attractions near the area. You can also choose according to your interests, so you can see what district may best fit your personality. If you want to know the best fit for you in every aspect – financial, proximity, ambiance and overall experience, check out the following recommended hotel areas or accommodation district on the next pages.

Chapter Four: Hotels and Accommodations

1. Prague 1 – The Old Town, The New Town, The Little Town, and Castle Town

The Prague 1 or district 1 is where the city – center is located. Since this is where four main towns in the city is located, you will definitely find all the best hotels, apartments, and other alternative accommodations.

The Old Town is the most popular place in Prague, you can find lots of 4 stars and 5 stars hotel as well as other cheaper accommodations. There are also plenty of restaurants around, and the hotels are usually up to 4 – story's high only.

Chapter Four: Hotels and Accommodations

If you wanted to have a view of the river, it's probably best to stay at the New Town. This is where the famous Wenceslas Square can be found, and also the hotspot for nightlife. Don't be surprised if there'll be lots of parties around. It's also an ideal place to those who loves shopping.

If you prefer to stay in a more quiet and serene place but still within the city – center, then the Little Town and Castle Town is where you should opt to stay. There are less clubs, and bars, less "noise," and perfect for those who are history buffs since it is near many historical places and landmarks. You can choose to stay in some of the oldest hotels and buildings around; restaurants also abound the area.

Here's a quick overview of the famous hotels around Prague 1:

The Old Town (Staré Město Pražské)

- Grand Hotel Praha
- The Emblem Hotel
- Hotel Černý Slon
- Hotel Dar
- Apartments Dusni – Old Town Square

Chapter Four: Hotels and Accommodations

The New Town (Nove Mesto)
- The Grand Mark Prague
- Hotel Exe City Hotel
- K+K Hotel Central Prague
- NYX Prague

The Little Town/ Lesser Town (Malá Strana)
- Design Metropol Hotel Prague
- Hotel Pod Vezi
- Golden Well Hotel
- Aparthotel City 5
- BoHo Prague Hotel

Castle Town (hotels nearest the Prague Castle)
- Miss Sophie's Hotel
- Questenberk
- Domus Henrici Boutique Hotel
- Hotel General
- Appia Hotel Residences

Chapter Four: Hotels and Accommodations

2. *Prague 2*

Prague 2 is the south – west area of central Prague that follows up the river, and only about 1 km away from Prague 1. This district also touches the eastern side of Prague.

The main area is called Vinohrady and Namesti Miru. This is a place that is relatively far from the city – center, but you can also find good apartments and hotels as well as independent bars, and boutiques. It's also just a few minute walk to other districts in Prague.

Chapter Four: Hotels and Accommodations

You can also find the famous Palac Flora Shopping Centre in this district. The street names in this district are cities and countries. It is also close to the New Jewish Cemetery.

Here's a quick overview of the famous hotels around the Prague 2:

- Mosaic House
- Park Inn Hotel Prague
- Hotel Galileo
- The Palace Suites and Apartments
- Novotel Praha Wenceslas Square
- Amigo City Centre Hotel
- Pension Brezine Prague
- Ibis Praha
- Residence La Fenice
- Royal Courts Apartments

Chapter Four: Hotels and Accommodations

3. *Prague 3*

Prague 3 starts at the Jiriho Podebrad Metro along the border of Vinohradska. It also touches the Prague 8 district and extends up to Prague 10 district in Vinohrady. This is mostly a residential district but there are also lots of accommodations around. The largest residential area you can visit is the Zizkov.

The Prague 8 side can be accessible by trams and buses; the Vinohradska side is where you can find several hotels and apartments. The area closest to district 2 is where

Chapter Four: Hotels and Accommodations

you can also find lots of cheap hotels that are just outside tourist centers. There are also local restaurants but not that many including boutiques and shops, but the good thing is that the other districts are all walking distance. Be prepared to walk for about half an hour or better yet use a public transportation for you to check different accommodation options in Prague 3.

Here's a quick overview of the famous hotels around Prague 3:

- Hotel Don Giovanni
- Marriott Courtyard Hotel
- Novum Hotel Vitkov
- Hotel Golden City
- City Lounge Hotel
- Vlkova Palace
- Hotel Taurus
- Hotel Residence Tabor
- Theatrino
- My Hotel Apollon

Chapter Four: Hotels and Accommodations

4. *Prague 4*

Another place close to river and not relatively far from the city – center is Prague 4. If you are really on a tight budget, this is the district where you can find both the cheapest and quite expensive hotels ranging from 3 stars to 4 stars. The highest concentrations of hotels are found in the Branik and Podoli area that are near the river. You can also find trams and bus services which makes this district also accessible.

Chapter Four: Hotels and Accommodations

Prague 4 like Prague 3 is also mostly a residential area; it also has train stations that runs from Vysehrad up to places called Opatov and Haje where many pensions and cheap hostels also abound. Make sure that you check the schedule of buses and check public transportation details so you can easily find the hotel you choose to stay otherwise you might end up spending more if you ride with taxis.

Here's a quick overview of the famous hotels around Prague 4:

- Panorama Hotel
- Corinthia Hotel
- Hotel Otakar
- Occidental Praha
- Hotel Nabucco
- Holiday Inn Hotel (Congress Centre)
- Hotel Michael
- Rezidence Vysehrad
- Vysehrad Hotel
- Villa Voyta Hotel

Chapter Four: Hotels and Accommodations

5. *Prague 5*

Another great place popular among tourists is the district of Prague 5 located in the southern ring road of the capital. Prague 5 extends from the Mala Strana River to the Zbraslav which is about 7 km to the south and extends to the airport from the castle's far side.

This district is semi – residential and is also semi – commercial. Prague 5 is the biggest district in the capital, and most hotels can be found in Andel and Ujezd area. The

Chapter Four: Hotels and Accommodations

last metro station in Prague 5 is called Smichov but it has been extended to Hlubocepy which is only a few minute walk if you are staying in Smaragd hotel.

Here's a quick overview of the famous hotels around Prague 5:

- Akcent Hotel
- Vienna House Hotel
- Lavanda Hotel & Apartments
- La Boutique Hotel
- Hotel Anette
- Aparthotel Angel
- Hotel Augustus et Otto
- Angel City Apartments
- Andel Apartments
- Lidicka Apartments

Chapter Four: Hotels and Accommodations

6. Prague 6

Prague 6 extends to the west and north of Castle Town to the boundaries of Prague 7. This is where you can find the main area called Dejvice which is the quickest connection that leads to the Prague Airport and the Dejvicka Metro Station. Aside from being a residential district, it's also filled with international and governmental institutions; this is where you can find several embassies or consulate offices of other countries. If you wish to stay in hotels closest to the airport or if you have a schedule at one of the embassies then Prague 6 is the district for you.

Chapter Four: Hotels and Accommodations

You won't be able to find many restaurants or bars as well as shops (except the shops found in the airport) and it is also quite far to the city – center and major tourist attractions.

Here's a quick overview of the famous hotels in Prague 6:

- Hotel Dakura
- Hotel Meda
- Hotel Three Storks
- Hotel Hoffmeister
- Residence Thunovska
- Hoffmeister Apartments
- EA Hotel Jeleni
- Waldstein Hotel
- At the Golden Plough Apartments
- Hotel Schwaiger

Chapter Four: Hotels and Accommodations

7. *Prague 7*

The district of Prague 7 is where you can find places called Liben and Holesovice that extends from the Letna River. This is also where you can find the National Prague Zoo called the Troja. If you choose to stay here, you can find various hotels in the Rivertown Market that are of good quality and also affordable. Many foreign tourists like to stay in Prague 7 because aside from having a cheap accommodation, the routes lead to the city – center, and public transportations are also easily accessible.

Chapter Four: Hotels and Accommodations

Here's a quick overview of the famous hotels in Prague 7:

- Parkhotel Praha
- Leon Hotel
- Extol Inn
- Comfortable Prague Apartments
- Art Hotel Prague
- Plaza Alta Hotel
- Hotel Klara
- Hotel Belvedere
- Absolutum Boutique Hotel
- Hotel Expo

Chapter Four: Hotels and Accommodations

8. Prague 8

The most popular place in Prague 8 is called Karlin and Kobylisy opposite the Vltava River. Major tourist attractions are easily accessible because for instance, if you will be staying in Karlin, you can just hop on a train that will lead you right to the Wenceslas and Republic Square.

For those staying in Kobylisy, you can also take the train station to take you to several tourist spots as well as the Mala Strana. Many hotels and accommodation hubs are concentrated near transportation stations. Lots of local dining places and a few boutiques here and there surround

Chapter Four: Hotels and Accommodations

the area. Karlin and Kobylisy are also walking distance from one another so you can easily check out various hotels and dining places.

Here's a quick overview of the famous hotels in Prague 8:

- Hotel Adeba
- 3D Apartments
- Pentahotel Prague
- Residence Casa Italia
- Hotel Charles Central
- Galerie Royale
- Hotel Royal
- Hotel Aaron
- Empirent Apartments
- Waterfront Apartments Prague

Chapter Four: Hotels and Accommodations

9. Prague 9

If you continued exploring in Prague 8, you'll eventually reach Prague 9. Unfortunately there aren't a lot of hotels here although there could be other accommodations like apartments or houses that are registered under Airbnb. Most tourists stay here if they will attend an event at the Ceskomoravska (O2 Arena). There are also many huge shopping centers and other commercial places. It is far from the city – center and places like bars, clubs or dining places are not abundant in this area unless there are major events.

Chapter Four: Hotels and Accommodations

Here's a quick overview of the famous in Prague 9:

- Wellness Hotel Step
- Habitat 16
- Hotel Carol
- Clarion Congress Hotel Prague
- EA Hotel Jasmin
- Duo
- Hotel Pivovar
- Hotel Arko
- Hotel Inturprag
- Hotel Relax Inn

Chapter Four: Hotels and Accommodations

10. Prague 10

Prague 10 borders with Pragues 2, 3, and 9. It is the last district in Prague before you enter the eastern side of the country particularly the Stredocesky district. You can find several train stations in Prague 10 including Zelivskeho, Strasnice and Skalka. The highest cluster of hotels and accommodations can be found in Strasnice particularly the Vrsovice Street. The hotels here are usually 3 – star hotels only which is perfect for those who are in a budget.

Prague 10 is also a residential district especially around the area of Zahradni Mesto (also known as Garden

Chapter Four: Hotels and Accommodations

Town). The main advantage in staying in this district is the public transportation – the metro trains and trams that are open and accessible 24/7 to take you to various places or the city – center.

Here's a quick overview of the famous hotels around Prague 10:

- Iris Hotel Eden
- Czech Inn
- Na Zamecku Hotel
- Hotel Aladin
- Hotel Mars
- Hotel Juno
- Hotel Jana
- Hotel Astra
- Pragueaparts Vinohrady
- Pension Hattrick

Chapter Four: Hotels and Accommodations

Chapter Five: Dining in Prague

Once you have decided what district you're going to stay in for your trip, the next thing on the list is your eating destination! Prague offers some of Europe's most savory dishes. In Prague, the local cuisine still holds a sacred place in the table; the city's dining culture is constantly evolving in a much slower pace compared to other European countries. Fortunately, Prague's traditional and classy dishes are still preferred by many. The city is keeping up with the changing palates through incorporating new modern flavors with their traditional dishes.

Chapter Five: Dining in Prague

In this chapter you will be given the top 10 restaurants that you need to dine in while you are in Prague, you will also be given a recommended list of other restaurants to ensure that you won't miss out the greatest gastronomic places that Prague has to offer.

1. Aromi

Aromi is a high – end Italian restaurant located in the residential area of Vinohrady. Make sure to reserve a table ahead of time if you're planning to dine here especially on the weekends. The place is packed every Friday and Saturday night. What both tourists and locals love about this restaurant is their sumptuous Italian dishes and of course, outstanding customer service.

Chapter Five: Dining in Prague

One of their specialties is the ravioli pasta, it's relatively cheaper if you order their pasta dishes topped with parmesan cheese or fried tuna. Aside from the cuisine, people love coming here because of the great ambiance that has a classy vibe – Italian style!

Here are other similar Italian restaurants in Prague you might want to check out:

- Wine O'Clock
- Ristorante Pagana
- La Botegga Linka
- La Finestra
- La Veranda
- Pastar Restaurant and Food Shop
- Alriso Risotteria Italiana
- Cicala Trattoria
- La Bottega Di Finestra
- Il Palazzo

2. *Bellevue*

If you are looking for a fancy restaurant on the riverside, then look no further because Bellevue can give you a nice view, and delicious Czech cuisine. People often come here because of the spectacular scenery. Aside from dining by the riverside, you can also see the beautiful Prague Castle which is perfect for couples who wanted to have a romantic dinner. It is quite expensive, and also considered as one of the most elegant tables in Prague. Diners can enjoy a two to five courses plus a wine – pairing menu (optional).

Chapter Five: Dining in Prague

The plating will surely increase your appetite, and the cuisine will make you forget your name! If you wanted to treat yourself with a loved one or a few friends, then splurge a little bit with Bellevue because it is surely worth it, and you'll have a great time, guaranteed!

Here are other similar fine dining restaurants in Prague you might want to check out:

- Alcron Restaurant
- V Zatisi
- Le Grill Restaurant
- Grand Cru
- Atelier Red & Wine
- Palffy Palac
- Terasa U Zlate studne
- Kampa Park
- Agave Restaurant
- Lal Qila – The Indian Restaurant

Chapter Five: Dining in Prague

3. *Blatouch*

Blatouch is located in the residential area of Vinohrady, it's a café bar that is perfect for students, acquaintances, and/or meetings. It's also walking distance from Namesti Miru. You can choose from a variety of sandwiches, pasta, salad dishes, and of course coffee or beer. The place has a great ambiance and very laid back. You can spend your afternoons here or have a conversation with a friend at night.

Here are other similar café bars in Prague you might want to check out:
- Jewel Café Bar
- Atmosfera Café Pub

Chapter Five: Dining in Prague

- Bukowski's
- Propaganda
- EMA Espresso Bar

4. *Café Imperial*

If you're looking for a more artsy type of coffee shop with a bit of historical ambiance, then head on over to Café Imperial. This café started in 1912, and it is one of the oldest coffee shops in the city. Although it was renovated a couple of years ago, the 20th century Art Nouveau vibe is still

Chapter Five: Dining in Prague

evident. The pillars and mosaics are still intact, but the overall quality of the restaurant is now modernized.

They don't only offer coffee, cakes, or pastas; you can also find Czech cuisine, and other international dishes. They also offer American breakfast, and a great spot to spend your mornings and afternoons.

Here are other similar coffee shops in Prague you might want to check out:

- LOCA Restaurant & Cafébar
- M&M Café Bar
- Café Lounge
- Kaldi
- Duende Café Bar

Chapter Five: Dining in Prague

5. Café Savoy

Another renovated coffeehouse from the 19th century is The Café Savoy. The ambiance and overall vibe of the restaurant will remind visitors of Imperial Vienna. The menu offered are Czech classics that you can eat for lunch or dinner. One of their best – sellers called Svíčková which is a traditional concoction of braised beef sirloin, served in gravy and topped with cranberry sauce; they also offer chicken breasts and pork meals for a reasonable amount. People often come here during the weekends as well as "brunch" because they also serve American and classic English

Chapter Five: Dining in Prague

breakfast. It's highly recommended that you reserve a table in advance.

Here are other similar coffee houses in Prague you might want to check out:

- Café Jen
- La Boheme Café
- Café No. 3
- Bella Vida Café
- Pražska Čokoládová Manufaktura
- Coffee Lovers
- Zmrzlina Créme de la Créme
- Garden Coffee Shop
- Cacao Prague
- Café Franz Kafka

Chapter Five: Dining in Prague

6. *Cukrkvalimonda*

This place is another famous coffee shop located in Mala Strana at the end of Charles Bridge. It is a rustic café restaurant that serves casual dining but may not be ideal for dinner because it closes quite early compared to other restaurants. People usually come here for lunch or in the afternoon. They offer salad and pasta dishes as well as pastry dishes like cakes and deserts paired with a cup of coffee.

Chapter Five: Dining in Prague

You should also book in advance, and make sure to bring only cash because they apparently don't accept credit cards.

Here are other coffee/pastry shops/restaurants in Prague that you should check out:

- Good Food Coffee & Bakery
- Paul
- Mannsson's Bakery
- Cukrarna Saint Tropez
- Cup and Cake
- Bistro Deli & Bakery
- Choco Loves Coffee
- Cakeshop Prague
- Ovocný Světozor
- Erhartova cukrárna

Chapter Five: Dining in Prague

7. *Hergetova - Cihelna*

Hergetova – Cihelna is a high – end and very fancy restaurant not only because of its exquisite menu but mostly because of its outstanding location. Tourists and locals alike come here because it offers the best riverside dining experience in Prague. They say that even the Holy Emperor, Charles IV will indeed dine here because of the great scenery, and a relaxing ambiance. Although they only offer casual snacks like pasta dishes, and a selection of burgers and sandwiches, this is still a hot spot for most tourists because of the riveting view. It's highly recommended that

Chapter Five: Dining in Prague

you reserve a table so you can get a terrace table and enjoy the view.

Here are some similar high – end restaurants in Prague that you need to check out:

- Restaurant Mlýnec
- George Prime Steak
- La Degustation Boheme Bourgeoise
- K The Two Brothers (Indian Restaurant)
- Field Restaurant
- Portfolio Restaurant
- The Grand Mark Prague
- Pagana
- Art & Food Had
- Boscolo Prague

Chapter Five: Dining in Prague

8. *Jahma*

If you had enough of the Czech cuisine and/or European dishes, why not taste the pride of the westerners with Jahma? This American restaurant, pronounced as "Yah-Ma" is also a pub located in the Lucerna shopping alley. The resto-bar offers the classic American dishes like steaks, burgers, Buffalo wings, nachos, Texas BBQ burgers, Tacos and the likes paired with beers and other drinks. They are mostly packed with young people, both Czech and foreign diners.

Here are some of the similar resto – bars in Prague:
- Cash Only Bar
- Spices Restaurant & Bar

Chapter Five: Dining in Prague

- Be Bop Bar Lobby
- Cloud 9 Sky Bar & Lounge
- James Dean Prague
- Merlin
- La Bodeguita Del Medio Music Bar & Restaurant
- Buddha-Bar Restaurant Prague
- Rocky O'Reilly's Irish Pub & Restaurant
- Popocafepetl - Újezd

9. Klub - Architekt

Klub – architect or Club of Architects is the most popular spot for architects and art design students back in the day. This is the go – to place if you wanted to taste various Czech dishes including braised pork tenderloin, and

Chapter Five: Dining in Prague

Prague goulash as well as potato dumplings, and the classic Czech Fried Cheese. You can dine and chill outside but during winter, the main dining room with a cozy ambiance is perfect for hanging out with friends and family.

Here are some similar themed restaurants in Prague that you can check out:

- Restaurace Kolonial
- Výtopna Railway Restaurant - Václavské náměstí
- Maitrea
- Bistro 8
- Naše maso
- The Tavern
- Bad Jeff's Barbeque
- U krále Brabantského
- Meat & Greet burgerhouse
- Letná Beer Garden

Chapter Five: Dining in Prague

10. U-Modr-Kachniky

U-Modr-Kachniky or the "Blue Duckling" is another hotspot for tourists and locals because of its gorgeous antique set – up, and one – of – a – kind Czech meal made up of roast duck stuffed with beer – plum sauce! Why not spend thanksgiving here? You can book a table at the upper floor so that you can also enjoy a piano background performance while you're eating with your loved ones. You might want to splurge in this restaurant especially if there'll be special occasions.

Chapter Five: Dining in Prague

Here are some similar restaurants you can go to in Prague for special occasions or events:

- In Loco
- Hostinec u Tunelu
- Santini Garden
- La Rotonde (Radisson Blu Alcron Hotel)
- Hostinec U Supa
- Mylnec
- Lokal
- U Vejvodu
- U Pinkasu Restaurant
- Pivnice u Lažanských

Chapter Five: Dining in Prague

Chapter Six: Tourist Destinations in Prague

Now that you have a basic idea about Prague, its people, and its culture, and now that you are fully equipped with the travelling essentials you may need before you go to this golden city, it's time to see the amazing landmarks that it has to offer! Like any other European countries, the City of a Hundred Spires is filled with history, tradition, and a full cultural experience. Be blown away and stand in awe as you see before you the various structures and historical spots that put the city "on the map."

Chapter Six: Tourist Spots in Prague

In this chapter, we will give you ten of the best historical and modern landmarks that Prague has to offer! You will learn a brief history about them, and its significance to the city. We also included the location details, some directions on how to get there, and the guided tours you can avail.

1. Charles Bridge

The most famous attraction in Prague is the Charles Bridge in honor of Holy Emperor, King Charles IV. It is established in the 14th century around 1357 by the King's favorite architect Perter Parler, the bridge links the two –

Chapter Six: Tourist Spots in Prague

sides of the capital. It is mainly constructed for knight tournaments back then, but today it is now a ceremonial bridge during important national events in Prague. It connects the Old Town, Little Town, and Castle Town. It is considered the busiest route, and one of the top tourist attractions in the city. Between the 1600 until the 1800 the Catholic Church erected 30 statues for ornamentation purposes.

The Charles Bridge is overlooking the beautiful and scenic Vltava River; it has a perfect view of the river as well as elegant structures on both sides. If you stroll down the bridge, you can see lots of musicians, street artists, and plenty of locals just enjoying the city. It's perfect for a romantic date early in the morning or late at night. The Charles Bridge starts at the Old Town Bridge Tower up to the Little Town or Lesser Town Bridge Tower.

Location/Directions:
The Charles Bridge is located in the Old Town Prague 1 connecting Mala Strana or the Lesser Town in the city – center.

Train station/s: Staromestska (line A; trams 2, 17, 18)

Tours: You can avail various guided tours around the city to learn more info about the Charles Bridge.

Chapter Six: Tourist Spots in Prague

2. Old Town Square

The Old Town Square dates back around 700 years ago, and it is a huge part of Prague's dramatic history and beginnings. It where you can find the most historical structures and sights in this city as well as architecturally mind – blowing church buildings. Back in the 12th century, it is the central market of Prague, and since then many buildings of Romanesque, Baroque, and Gothic styles has been erected. You can find many tourist spots in Old Town Square including the Old Town Hall Tower, the Tyn Church, and the Astronomical Clock among many.

Chapter Six: Tourist Spots in Prague

The Jan Hus statue is that dates back in 1915 is also erected here. You can enjoy the locals, tourists, and sights around by spending an afternoon with a cup of coffee; there are also many fine dining, and several shops as well as marketplace to buy from.

Location: Old Town Square, Old Town, Prague 1, Czech Republic

Train Station/s: Staromestska (line A; trams 2, 17, 18), Namesti Republiky (line B), Mustek (lines A & B)

Tours: You can avail various guided tours and/or bike tours around the Old Town Square to learn more info about this historical place.

3. Prague Castle

The Prague Castle is another major tourist attraction in all of Europe. It was once a seat of a Bohemian King during the medieval times. Today, this is where the President of the Czech Republic resides. It is located in Hradčany or the Castle District just above the Little/Lesser Town. The castle covers about 18 acres or 7 hectares of land. This is also where you can find St. Vitus Cathedral which is considered as the most dominant and recognizable

Chapter Six: Tourist Spots in Prague

landmark in Prague, although many people or tourists mistake it as the Prague Castle.

The castle went through lots of renovations over the years because of various factors such as fires, wars, and political agenda as well as military forces. The castle is also surrounded with other structures such as halls, monasteries, towers, museums, art galleries, state apartments as well as the so - called Golden Lane.

Many tourists check out the courtyards as well as the famous St. Vitus Cathedral. It is highly recommended that you avail the castle tour so that you can truly appreciate the history behind this great and magnificent landmark. You can also choose to purchase a ticket for each structure inside the castle complex.

Location: 119 08 Prague Castle Prague 1, Czech

Train Station/s: Malostranska (line A); Prazsky hrad or Pohorele (tram 22)

Tours: You can choose three different sections of tours so you can tour around the whole Prague Castle complex.

Chapter Six: Tourist Spots in Prague

4. Dancing House

Nicknamed as Fred and Ginger, the Dancing House is one of the most modernized buildings in Prague. Its architecture and overall design is very striking, and although it is a modern type of structure, it still has a historic architecture. The building began its construction in 1992, and it was completely finished in 1996. The curvy outlines of the building made its architects, Vlado Milunic and Frank

Chapter Six: Tourist Spots in Prague

Gehry, called it the Fred and Ginger building - it was name after the dance duo at the time.

The top-most floor of the building is the only part that is open to the public; this is another food hub for tourists because the Ginger and Fred restaurant is located here. The restaurant offers an international menu plus a great view of the city overlooking Charles Bridge and other beautiful sights of Prague.

Location: Dancing House
Jiraskovo namesti, New Town, Prague 2, Czech Republic

Train Station/s: Karlovo namesti (line B); Jiraskovo namesti (trams 5, 17)

You can avail a tour at this website:

<www.getyourguide.com/dancing-house>

Chapter Six: Tourist Spots in Prague

5. Estates Theater

The Estates Theater is officially opened to the public in 1783. It is one of Europe's oldest and most historical theaters. Its magnificent neo - classical structure is a must - see especially for those who love theatre and performing arts. The whole building echoes all the greatest and most talented musicians and performers, playwrights, and directors who ever lived. This is where Wolfgang Mozart, one of the world's greatest musician and composer, debut his masterpiece called Don Giovanni.

Chapter Six: Tourist Spots in Prague

Mozart lived in Prague where he crafted many operas performed in the Estates Theater. His another masterpiece called the Marriage of Figaro debuted in Vienna but it became wildly successful in Prague which is why he was commisssioned to create Don Giovanni in the city and conducted its world - premiere in Estates Theater in1787.

Since then, Mozart and other several musical geniuses and playwrights regularly performed in Estates Theater. Today the theater runs Mozart's Don Giovanni opera everyday starting from July up to August. The theater oftentimes runs a "Mozzartissimo" which is like a marathon of all of Mozart's famous operas and musical performances.

Location: Estates Theatre, Ovocny trh 1, Old Town, Prague 1, Czech Republic

Train Station/s: Mustek (lines A & B); Namesti Republiky (trams 6, 8, 15, 26)

You can avail tickets at this website:

<https://www.estatestheatre.cz>

Chapter Six: Tourist Spots in Prague

6. *The Powder Gate*

The powder gate dates back to 11th century, it is one of the main entrances in the old town of Prague. Construction began around 1475 during King Vladislav's reign. It was patterned after the bridge of the Old Town Tower. The gate's original name was the New Tower, but during the 17th century it was referred to as the Powder Tower or Powder Gate because it is where gunpowder is stored for battles/wars.

Chapter Six: Tourist Spots in Prague

Today, tourists can climb up the 186 stairs to see the Prague Towers art exhibition created by Ladislav Sitensky. Once you reached the top you can enjoy the scenic view of the Old Town and other famous landmarks in Prague. If you want to gomin depth of Powder Gate's historical significance, you can avail a general Prague tour offered by various tourism facilities.

Location: Powder Gate, Republic Square, Old Town, Prague 1, Czech Republic

Train Station/s: Namesti Republiky (line B; trams 6, 8, 15, 26)

You can avail tickets at this website:

<https://www.czechopera.cz/theatre-Estates_Theatre-schedule-3>

Chapter Six: Tourist Spots in Prague

7. *Municipal House*

Another Art Nouveau structure in the city is the Municipal House. It has the largest and perhaps one of the grandest concert halls in Prague and in Europe. It has many rooms, and you can also dine in elegant French restaurants, high - end coffee shops, beer - style hall restaurants and its first American bar offering the best of Czech cuisine. It also has plenty of exhibition rooms and salons.

It officially opened to the public in 1912, built at the former site of the Royal Court palace. Around 1918, the

Chapter Six: Tourist Spots in Prague

Czech Republic's proclamation of independence from Czechoslovakia happened in the Municipal House.

The Republic Square is the house's main attraction; other tourist spots like the Old Town Square, the Powder Gate, and the Wenceslas Square are all walking distance from here.

The building has an intricate designs made up of frescoes, glass windows, and gold trimmings. It also has a marble staircase that will take you to another architectural masterpiece called the Smetana Concert Hall. Smetana Hall takes pride not only in its marvelous and grand architecture but also the largest and most famous orchestras that played there. The Municipal House is home to the Czech National Symphony Orchestra; perhaps the best that Prague can offer always play and rehearse here.

Location: Address of Municipal House, Municipal House Republic Square 5, Old Town, Prague 1, Czech Republic

Train Station/s: Namesti Republiky (line B; trams 6, 8, 15, 26)

You can avail tickets and/or tours at this website:

<www.obecnidum.cz/en/ticket-sales-and-guided-tours-1404042442.html>

8. The Astronomical Clock and Old Town Hall Tower

This clock is perhaps one of the grandest, most complex and oldest clocks in the world. It dates back to the 15th century, it does not only tell time, but also the date, the zodiac sign, the feasts of saint and other important dates that is significant to Prague.

Tourists from all over the world often gather here to watch the 12 Apostle's procession on top every hour. A small door opens up as Jesus Christ and his apostles'

Chapter Six: Tourist Spots in Prague

marches out. You can also see a so called skeleton of death as it rings the bell to a Turk's statue.

After gazing at the Astronomical clock, you can head on over to the Old Town Hall Tower, this tower was erected in 1338, and you can climb to its top using an elevator or a staircase. The views are awe - inspiring because you can overlook the whole Old Town Square filled with locals and tourists alike and oversee other landmarks. It was also renovated around 1470 and remodeled into a Gothic style structure. Today the Old Town Hall is where Prague's Tourist Center is located, and it also holds various civic activities.

Location: Old Town Hall Tower & Astronomical Clock Old Town Square, Old Town, Prague 1, Czech Republic

Train Station/s: Staromestska (line A; trams 2, 17, 18)

You can avail guided tours at this website:

<www.getyourguide.com/prague-astronomical-clock-l3554>

9. Wenceslas Square

The Wenceslas Square is a favorite spot of tourists because aside from being a historical place, many hotels, banks, shops, bars/clubs and restaurants are located here. It is one of the commercial districts of Prague and it is also the center of nightlife in the city. It's also only a few minutes away from the Old Town Square as well as other main tourist destinations in Prague, and transportation services are highly accessible.

Chapter Six: Tourist Spots in Prague

The square is about 750 meters long and 60 meters wide. It was a horse market about 600 years ago.

Another major significance of the Wenceslas Square is that this is where all the Czech's rally and gather whenever they wanted to send off a message to their government. It also holds various political agendas, organizational gatherings, and where sporting achievements are celebrated. It can hold up to 40,000 people.

It is also near the National Museum and the Prague State Opera. You will get to see the remarkable yet intriguing statue of St. Wenceslas who were once a king but unfortunately was murdered by his own brother. He became the Czech's patron saint, which is why the square was named after him.

Location: Wenceslas Square, New Town, Prague 1, Czech Republic

Train Station/s: Muzeum (lines A & C), Mustek (lines A & B), Vaclavske namesti (trams 3, 5, 6, 9, 14, 24)

You can avail guided tours at this website:

<https://www.getyourguide.com/wenceslas-square-14829>

Chapter Six: Tourist Spots in Prague

10. *Vltava River*

The Vltava River is hard to miss because it is the most natural attraction that connects the city of Prague to the rest of the Czech Republic; it is where the city developed for the past thousands of years.

You can find the Old Town, and the New Town on one side, while the Mala Strana (Little/ Lesser Town) and Castle Town lies on the other side. The panoramic view from the Charles Bridge is a great opportunity for awesome photo - op. You can also avail a river cruise tour that will give you

Chapter Six: Tourist Spots in Prague

a scenic and refreshing view of the city. You can see lots of swans and birds around and oversee the Petrin hills.

The Vltava River plays a significant role and it pretty much founded the great city of Prague. This is where most natives and locals get their water for drinking and irrigation which enabled early settlements around the area and eventually developed into a city we now know today. It is also the main pathway that leads to the Southern and Northern parts of Europe that provided access for trade and commerce back in the day.

The Vltava River measures about 430 km but because of its strong current, large canals and dams were built to make navigation easier, and make transportation of goods and people more safe and accessible. It now flows to the River of Elbe, and it is the longest river in the Czech Republic, and one of the most scenic natural bodies of water in all of Europe.

Location: Vltava River, Prague, Czech Republic

Train Station/s: Staromestska (line A; trams 2, 17, 18)

You can avail a river cruise/ tour at this website:
<http://www.prague-boats.cz/river-cruises>

Chapter Six: Tourist Spots in Prague

Chapter Seven: Religious Places in Prague

Europe is the center of many religions in the world, and Prague is one of those cities that offer many worship places that stood the test of time. The city boasts its grand church towers, basilicas, and synagogues with different combination of architectural forms, and designed by the Czech Republic's most renowned artists.

In this chapter we will give you ten of the best churches, basilicas, synagogues, and other religious structures in Prague that many Catholics and Jews can drop by and worship in as well as a great photo opportunity for tourists of other faiths.

Chapter Seven: Religious Places in Prague

1. Tyn Church

Also known as The Church of Our Lady Before Tyn is the most elegant Gothic church (with a Baroque interior) in Prague that is located in Old Town Square. It is founded in 1385, and it was the main church in Old Town, and in all of Prague. It was formerly under the control of Hussites, around the 15th century, but it is because at the time they were being killed by Catholics. The Catholic Jesuits eventually took over the church, and they replaced the chalice of the Hussites with a figurine of Mary, they also re-casted the bell.

Chapter Seven: Religious Places in Prague

The church was caught in fire in 1679 which led to its interior renovation of a Baroque style, but the exterior remains purely Gothic. The towers of the church are a representation of Adam and Eve or the masculine/feminine sides at the time of the Gothic period. The tower stands at about 80 meters, and it is not symmetrical.

It was told that Walt Disney got the idea and inspiration of the Sleeping Beauty Castle through the towers of the Tyn Church. The church also houses the oldest organ in Prague that dates back to 1673. The Tyn Church holds regular Eucharistic celebrations as well as other church services; it also holds various events like classical concerts.

Location: Tyn Church, Old Town Square, Old Town, Prague 1, Czech Republic

Train Station/s: Staromestska (line A); Namesti Republiky (line B); Namesti Republiky (trams 6, 8, 15, 26)

Chapter Seven: Religious Places in Prague

2. St. Vitus Cathedral (Katedrála svatého Víta)

St. Vitus Catheral is most of the time mistaken as the Prague Castle because of its grand exterior, and because it is located inside the Prague Castel complex. Its dominating structure can be seen from afar in the city – center. The St. Vitus Cathedral is also a masterpiece of Gothic architecture, and it spiritually symbolizes the Czech Republic.

King Charles commissioned the cathedral, and it began building around the 10th century but it took more than 5 centuries, and was finally finished in 1929. It was constructed by Matthias and Peter Parler (who built the Charles Bridge and King Charles' favorite architect). You can

Chapter Seven: Religious Places in Prague

also find the Golden Portal, and the St. Wenceslas Chapel which is crafted with previous stones, and decorated with frescoes. The chapel also houses the Bohemian Coronation Jewels. Aside from that you can also visit the Royal Mausoleum, Royal Tombs and Crypts inside the church. St. Vitus Cathedral is also where royalties of the Czech Republic held its coronation ceremonies.

You can also check out 14th century – old Great South Tower (about 90 meters high) which holds the largest bell in the whole country. Tourists can climb up the 287 steps to enjoy the spectacular view of the city, and also see the Zikmund (bell).

Location: St. Vitus Cathedral at Prague Castle
Prague Castle, Castle District, Prague 1, Czech Republic

Train Station/s: Malostranska (line A), Prazsky hrad or Pohorelec (tram 22)

Chapter Seven: Religious Places in Prague

3. St. Nicholas Church of Old Town Square

St. Nicholas Church located in the Old Town Square is a replacement to a small parish Church around 1273. Its construction was finished in 1735, and it also one of Prague's pride in terms of Baroque architecture.

The interior was patterned after the chapel in Paris called Chapel of St. Louis-des-Invalides; the Baroque design is done by Bernardo Spinetti as well as the church's stucco décor. There are also beautiful frescoes created by Peter Adam, and magnificent sculptures made by Antonin Braun.

Chapter Seven: Religious Places in Prague

Around 1781, several monasteries including the St. Nicholas' Church was shut down by Emperor Josef II prohibiting all church activities and social functions. The church eventually became a Russian Orthodox around 1870.

At the time of the Second World War, Czech military forces restored the church with the help of various artists. St. Nicholas Church eventually was under the supervision of the Czech Hussites until today. In 1901, the Krenn House that is in – front of the church was demolished which paved the way for the world to see the stunning beauty of St. Nicholas' Church. It holds various church activities, holy mass, as well as musical concerts.

Location: St. Nicholas Church Old Town Square
Old Town Square, Old Town, Prague 1, Czech Republic

Train Station/s: Staromestska (line A; trams 2, 17, 18)

Chapter Seven: Religious Places in Prague

4. Strahov Monastery (Strahovské nádvoří)

The Strahov Monastery is located behind the Prague Castle and the Petrin Hill. It was erected in 1140, and founded by Prince Vladislav II. The monastery was originally built for the followers of St. Augustine called the Premonstretensians. Around 1258, the monastery was completely destroyed due to a fire which led to its reconstruction to a Gothic style architecture that carried on until the Baroque period.

If you go to Strahov Monastery, you'll be able to appreciate the serene and meditative atmosphere of the place, and also get to enjoy the view of the Little Town and other parts of the city. It also houses some of the oldest monastic book collections with over 16,000 books collected in the past centuries from theological to philosophical references.

Location: Strahov Monastery, Strahovske nadvori 1, Strahov, Castle District, Prague 1, Czech Republic

Train Station/s: Malostranska (line A); Pohorelec (tram 22)

Chapter Seven: Religious Places in Prague

5. St. Peter and Paul Church

The St. Peter & Paul Church is located at the top of Vysehrad overlooking the Vltava River. It was founded 70 years after the Prague Castle was built. It also serves as a trading post back in the day. The church's interior had been renovated over the years, and ever since it was open to the public many tourists and devotees come here to pray and worship.

The church's location in the Vysehrad Park goes way back in 1085. Also known as Castle on the Heights, the park was established by a Bohemian royalty named Prince Vratislav II.

Chapter Seven: Religious Places in Prague

After visiting the beautiful church of St. Peter and Paul, you can stroll around the former castle complex and visit the beautiful gardens or have a picnic with your family while appreciating the scenic view of the Vltava River.

Aside from the church and the calm oasis of the Vysehrad Park, you can also visit the burial place of many of the country's notable artists, architects, designers, and musicians as well as politicians, and other important people including Antonín Dvořák, Bedřich Smetana and Alfons Mucha. After a long walk, why not take a rest at coffee shops around the area while admiring the 11th century - old St. Martin's Rotunda, another great landmark in Prague that depicts Czech Mythology.

Location: St. Peter & Paul Church V Pevnosti 5b, Vysehrad, Prague 2, Czech Republic

Train Station/s: Vysehrad (line C); Vyton (trams 3, 7, 16, 17); Albertov (trams 7, 8, 24)

Chapter Seven: Religious Places in Prague

6. St. George's Basilica at Prague Castle (Bazilika Sv. Jiří)

St. George's Basilica is one of the most preserved churches in all of Europe, it is also the oldest Romanesque church structure in Prague, and it is located inside the Prague Castle complex. The basilica was established in 920 by Prince Vratislav. Around 973, the St. George's Benedictine Convent was added as part of the church.

A destructive fire destroyed the original basilica in 1142, it was then renovated to a Baroque façade, and construction

Chapter Seven: Religious Places in Prague

was completed in 1691. Its interior is made up of deep woods, and has decorative windows that provide a lighted atmosphere. According to many tourists, the design and overall effect feels as if you've been transported to an old or ancient world. You can also see various paintings in the altar as well as frescos created by Reiner.

The church is also where tombs of historical and religious people of Prague lie including St. Ludmila, Prince Boleslav II, and Prince Vratislav. You can also attend classical concerts at night or simply marvel at the building's Romanesque structure, and romantic setting.

Location: St. George's Basilica at Prague Castle
Prague Castle, Castle District, Prague 1, Czech Republic

Train Station/s: Malostranska (line A), Prazsky hrad or Pohorelec (tram 22)

7. *Spanish Synagogue*

The Spanish Synagogue is buried in the Jewish Quarter of Prague, it is considered as one of the most magnificent worship places in Europe, and also the most beautiful synagogue in Prague.

Built in 1868 by Vojtěch Ignátz Ullmann and designed in a Moorish style, the Spanish Synagogue has a stained glass window, and arabesque low stucco interior that was finished around 1893, and it was also the former site of a Jewish house of prayer called The Old Shul.

Chapter Seven: Religious Places in Prague

During the communist rule and World Wars, the Spanish Synagogue was closed and destroyed. Fortunately, around the latter part 20th century after the chaos, it was handed over to the Jewish Museum and was rebuilt to the structure we now see today. It is now part of the Jewish Museum's building, and it also holds classical concerts from time to time as well as Jewish ceremonies.

Location: Spanish Synagogue
Vezenska 1, Josefov, Prague 1, Czech Republic

Train Station/s: Staromestska (line A); Pravnicka fakulta (tram 17)

Chapter Seven: Religious Places in Prague

8. Old New Synagogue

The Old New Synagogue is also one of the oldest Jewish synagogues in all of Europe. It is located in Josefov which is the city's former Jewish Quarter. It was erected in 1270, and legend has it that the stones to build the synagogue's walls was brought to the city by angels. Religious activities were stopped during the Second World War because the city was occupied by Nazi's.

Another legend surrounding the Old New Synagogue is that during the 16th century, Jewish Rabbi Jehud Löwa created a golem out of clay, and breathes life into it.

Chapter Seven: Religious Places in Prague

The Golem became angry and aggressive which is why the Rabbi returned him to clay. According to Jewish teachings, it means that when the Jewish faith is in trouble, the Golem will return again.

Location: Maiselova, Josefov, Prague 1, Czech Republic

Train Station/s: Praha - Bubny

Chapter Seven: Religious Places in Prague

9. *The Church of Our Lady Victorious*

Tucked away in the Little/ Lesser Town in Prague, the Church of Our Lady Victorious is a place where devotees and tourists alike loves to go to. It was the first ever Baroque church built in the city. The structure is covered in marble and gold, and its overall ambiance is luxurious like a 5 – star hotel! Many tourists and locals love to come here because they consider the church as a hidden luxury. Aside from the magnificent structure, people also come here to see the wax figure of Jesus Christ as a baby, also known as the Infant of Prague. You can also check out a display of Baby Jesus'

gowns and dresses given by royalties, and notable personalities from the past centuries.

Location: Karmelitská 9, Praha 1, Czech Republic

Train Station/s: Malostranske namesti (tram no. 22, 12)

10. St. Salvator Church

St. Salvator Church can easily be seen because it is located at the Charles Bridge. It also has an incredible façade and magnificent interior structure that will encourage any tourist walking at the bridge to visit.

Chapter Seven: Religious Places in Prague

The St. Salvator Church also has some historical significance to the city because it is the former residence of Jesuit priests. It is also one of the earliest Baroque structures in Prague, and it houses two huge organs. Over the years, the church underwent renovation, and aside from church activities, it also holds opera and musical concerts all year round.

Location: Křižovnické náměstí, 110 00 Staré Město, Czechia

Train Station/s: Staromestska (trams 2, 17, 18)

Chapter Eight: Museums in Prague

Prague is also home to some of the most ancient relics and unknown artifacts in Central Europe. The city's museum and art galleries are perfect for history buffs and religious devotees, and even those who are interested in ancient things and architecture. Prague doesn't only offer ancient exhibits found inside the museums, the city also takes pride in its world – renowned architecture which is considered as a masterpiece by many locals; it will feel like you're walking in a real – life museum! In this chapter, you'll be provided with ten of the best museums and art galleries in Prague along with the essential details you need about it.

Chapter Eight: Museums in Prague

1. National Museum (Narodni Muzeum)

The National Museum of Prague is the biggest and oldest museum not just in Prague but in the whole country. It has two buildings consisting of both the old and new. The old building has a classic neo – Renaissance architecture, but it was recently renovated. The new building was home to the Czechoslovakia parliament back in 1989 as well as the Radio Free Europe sometime after the communist era. There new building holds over 20 million historical objects but only a few of them are being shown or exhibited. It also holds temporary exhibits for visitors and was also used as

Chapter Eight: Museums in Prague

the permanent storage house of various artifacts given to the National Museum

Location: National Museum, Wenceslas Square 68, New Town, Prague 1, Czech Republic
Tel. Number: +420 224 497 111
Website: www.nm.cz

2. Villa Amerika Dvorak Museum

Located inside the National Museum complex is the the Dvorak Museum was established in 1932, and it is also home to Villa Amerika.

Chapter Eight: Museums in Prague

It was originally built as a summer house back in the 18th century which is why the building has a magnificent Baroque style of architecture. You can also see frescoes on the wall that makes up the structure's interior design.

The Dvorak museum holds several exhibits and shows that is dedicated to Antonin Dvorak, he was the pride of the Czech Republic because he's the first Czech composer, and one of the best chamber musical and oratory composers in Europe. He is also an acclaimed musician that gained international recognition, and became one of the musical directors in New York's National Conservatory of Music for three years in a row.

Location: Villa Amerika Dvorak Museum
Ke Karlovu 20, Vinohrady, Prague 2, Czech Republic
Tel. Number: +420 224 923 363
Website: www.nm.cz/

Chapter Eight: Museums in Prague

3. St. Vitus Cathedral Museum

Aside from being one of Prague's most renowned churches, its museum also holds some of the most important religious relic and historical artifacts in Europe. As mentioned earlier, this is the place where Bohemian Kings are crowned back in the day, which is why the museum is also filled with various crowning jewels, tombs of notable royalties as well as other important paintings. The museum is part of the Prague Castle complex tour, you can also just avail the St. Vitus Cathedral tour so you can learn more about Prague's history.

Location: St. Vitus Cathedral at Prague Castle
Prague Castle, Castle District, Prague 1, Czech Republic
Website: http://www.katedralasvatehovita.cz/cs

4. Lobkowicz Palace and Museum

The Prague Castle complex is considered a real life museum in itself because you can see many major tourist attractions but each of them houses important historical artifacts. Aside from that it is also a remarkable place

Chapter Eight: Museums in Prague

because this is where the President of the Czech Republic resides. You can see lots of exhibitions, art galleries, and various events taking place as well as landmarks inside the complex including the Lobkowicz Palace and Museum.

The Lobkowicz Palace and Museum houses world – renowned collections from various artists including Beethoven, Mozart, and Haydn's several original manuscripts (from 17th – 19th century), paintings by Velasquez, Brueghel, Canaletto as well as a vast collections of armories from many centuries ago.

The Lobkowicz Palace and Museum is the #1 pick of travel site TripAdvisor for 2 years in a row (2015 – 16)! For you to know more about the history of Prague and make the most out of your trip to the castle complex why not take an official tour which also includes a visit to other landmarks like the Golden Lane, Powder Gate, St. George's Basilica and the stunning Royal Palace.

Location: Jiřská 3, Praha 1 – Hradčany, Czech Republic

Tel. Number: +420 233 312 925

Website: www.lobkowicz.cz/

Chapter Eight: Museums in Prague

5. *Charles Bridge Museum*

The Charles Bridge museum is quite hidden in Krísovnické námestí. And it tells the historical significance of Prague's most famous bridge that connects the city ever since the era of King Charles. You'll see permanent exhibits that tell the story of how destructive floods destroyed the Judith Bridge which was the first ever bridge built in Vltava River. You can actually walk down the steps of the Judith Bridge's original stonework that dates back to the 12th century.

Chapter Eight: Museums in Prague

You'll also learn how the famed Charles Bridge was built through various carpentry and masonry techniques used by the builders and architects. There is a star exhibit where you can see the scale model of the bridge that took about more than one year to build. An interesting thing to find out is that if King Charles actually ordered egg yolks and add it to the mortar that bonds the bricks together.

Location: Křižovnické náměstí Praha 1, Czech Republic

Tel. Number: +420 603 819 947

Website: www.prague-bridge.com/

Chapter Eight: Museums in Prague

6. *The Museum of Communism*

Established by an American entrepreneur named Glenn Spicker, the Museum of Communism houses the artifacts collected during the Communist era from junk shops to various market fleas. Once you visit this museum, you'll see a glimpse of how people lived through the suppression and fear because of the Communist ruling that lasted for over 40 years until 1989. There are three rooms in the museum namely; the Communist Dream, The Reality, and The Nightmare. The rooms were creatively arranged to depict the reality of how it all went down during the Communist era.

Chapter Eight: Museums in Prague

You'll also see an exhibit that has the photo of Stalin monument and it shows Stalin leading his military forces in Letna Park; Josef Stalin is the Russian dictator that occupied the Czech Republic during World War II.

The Stalin Monument was the largest statue in Europe back in the day but when Josef Stalin was accused of committing homicide that's why in 1962, the Russian government decided to blow up the monument.

Location: Na Příkopě 10, 110 00 Nové Město, Czechia

Tel. Number: +420 224 212 966

Website: www.muzeumkomunismu.cz/

7. *Irish Museum of Modern Art*

The Irish Museum of Modern Art is located outside the city – center but despite of its quite remote location, many art lovers and tourists come here because of the modern art it offers. The museum is erected in a 17th century old court yard, and it also holds many open – air fests with an amazing and creative art background. Most of the Irish artists who contributed in various contemporary artworks exhibited in the museum are unknown to many, so just let their artworks speak for itself.

Chapter Eight: Museums in Prague

8. DOX Centre for Contemporary Arts

For those who love modern art, the DOX Centre for Contemporary Arts is a great place to spend your weekends. The art gallery museum located in Holesovice neighborhood in Prague 7 houses many timeless political arts in the city. You can find many exhibits as well as curated art works. Art enthusiasts love coming to this art gallery even on weekdays.

You won't miss the DOX's building because its façade is painted with creative murals and the structure is also covered with quotes from famous people translated to Czech language.

Chapter Eight: Museums in Prague

Location: Poupětova 1, Praha 7, Czechia

Tel. Number: +420 295 568 123

Website: www.dox.cz

9. Old Sewage Works Eco – Technical Museum

The Old Sewage Works museum was the capital's main sewage system until 1967. An English man named, Engr. William Lindley built the brick vaulted sewers from 1881 to 1889. Today, it is now an Eco – technical museum!

Chapter Eight: Museums in Prague

It's also considered a national monument, and a one – of – a – kind experience for visitors and locals especially those who are engineers and builders

Location: Papirenska 199/6, Papírenská 6, Prague 160 00, Czech Republic
Tel. Number: +420 777 790 219

10. Mucha Museum

The Mucha Museum is dedicated to Alfonse Mucha which is one of Prague's most outstanding Art Nouveau artists during the 20th century; he was also famous for

Chapter Eight: Museums in Prague

creating the best and most artistic theater poster ads during his time. His famous works are exhibited in the museum including his stage play called Gismonda, you'll also see lots of panels, menus, calendars, magazine covers, stamps, postcards and banknotes that he himself designed.

He also designed various jewelries and tableware items which were also published as a book. The Mucha Museum also holds some of Alfonse's personal belongings, candid photos of him and his models as well as the other artworks he made in his career.

Location: Kaunický Palác, Panská 7, 110 00 Nové Město, Czechia
Tel. Number: +420 224 216 415
Website: www.mucha.cz

Chapter Nine: Nightlife in Prague

If you're not a morning person or you don't like to roam around this beautiful city with a whole crowd of tourists behind you then perhaps you are better off wandering at night! Prague offers a variety of choices on how to enjoy the night life that aren't just limited in going to clubs or bars. You can have lots of options where you can relax, enjoy, and have the best time with your loved ones. Prague turns into both a romantic place and a party hub at night with the best cuisines, the best drinks, the best views, and the best people to have fun with! Here are ten of the best bars, clubs, and fun themed places you can spend your night in.

Chapter Nine: Nightlife in Prague

1. Club *Sasazu*

Sasazu is the latest party club in Prague. Many international and local DJs have come here, and lots of locals and tourists who love house music are the usual customers. It officially opened in 2009, and since then many famous artists, and musicians have come here including One Republic, Paul Van Dyk, Fedde Le Grand and Tiesto among

Chapter Nine: Nightlife in Prague

many. Its venue can hold more than 2,500 people, and it is considered as one of the biggest nightclub in the city.

Sasazu's is a huge entertainment facility with a dance floor located in its center surrounded by different kinds of bars in every corner! You can also hang out with your friends at the upper deck or the balcony because it offers a more private space and a nice view of people partying on the dance floor. The best time to go clubbing in Sasazu is every Saturday night.

Cost: Tables cost around 200 CZK or around $10 or more especially if there is a major event or famous/international performers. Drinks are relatively expensive depending on the kind of beer you want to drink.

Location: Bubenske nabrezi 306/13 17004 Prague, Czech Republic Holesovice (North of the Vltava River)

Chapter Nine: Nightlife in Prague

2. *The Retro Club*

    The Retro club is one of the best electro music clubs in the city, its venue can hold more than 1,200 people, and many famous DJs also play here every weekend. Retro is like Sasazu but relatively smaller, though the music and experience could be greater. It also has an upper deck and a dance floor at its center. There are also lots of mini-bars, and a separate table section if you prefer a bit of privacy.

    The main difference between Sasazu Club and the Retro club is that the latter has an incredible sound system, the music is way louder, and the light show is also spectacular, it's like you're attending a concert, dancing your

Chapter Nine: Nightlife in Prague

heart out in a club, and drinking the best spirits in a bar – all in one! There are also many tourists and locals who come here every night.

Cost: Entrance fee for male customers are around $5 but female customers are free of charge. The drinks are at a reasonable price, and it is not that expensive since it's not located or near major tourist spots.

3. *Karlovy Lázně*

Karlovy Lázně is the biggest (or perhaps the tallest) music venue not just in Prague but in all of Central Europe. It has 5 floors where each floor has a different music theme including, hip – hop music, electric music or EDM, 80's dance floor, hard – core trance floor, as well as mellow entertainment room (located on the top floor) among many.

Chapter Nine: Nightlife in Prague

What's more interesting is the incredible 14th century design of the building's interior. The floors and walls are covered with mosaic tiles which give the whole building a classic yet vibrant vibe. It is also the hub of many foreigners and fellow tourists from around the world. This club is one of the most must – see and must – experience club in Prague and in Europe! Every night at Club Karlovy Lázně is a night to remember!

Cost: Entrance cost somewhere between 150 - 200 CZK or $7 - 10 per pax. Drinks can be very expensive since it's located in a tourist part of town.

Location: Novotneho Lavka 5 Old Town, Prague 1 (just right next to Charles Bridge; you can take the tram and hop off the Karlovy Lazne station

Chapter Nine: Nightlife in Prague

4. *Lucerna*

Lucerna is the best place for those who are a bit older, especially for tourists who love the 80's and 90's music! It's also a huge but underground club that hosts many local bands every week, and then turns into a sort of "throwback" party club every Friday and Saturday (since local bands perform in the venue every week).

You can see huge TV screens that plays the music video of each 80's/ 90's song, and you can also rock your heart out in its huge dance floor. Lucerna is also famous

Chapter Nine: Nightlife in Prague

among international students and expats. It's a great place to meet new and probably interesting people!

Cost: Entrance costs 200 CZK or $5 for guys, while women are free. Drinks are also reasonably price, and its bar has a wide selection of authentic Czech spirits, beer and other international liquors.

Location: Vodickova 36, New Town, Prague 1 (Once you're in the Wenceslas Square at night, you can see a huge neon sign of Lucerna)

Chapter Nine: Nightlife in Prague

5. *Duplex*

Another club that is located in Wenceslas Square is called Duplex. Duplex is a club that has the best location in Prague because it is on a rooftop. Aside from night clubbing, you and your loved ones can also enjoy a great lunch and dinner at its resto-bar.

The clubs interior looks like a very big glass cube and the views on top are awesome. It has two dance floors located on different levels, four bars, and of course, an incredible sound system.

Chapter Nine: Nightlife in Prague

Duplex Club received recognition as one of the World's Finest Clubs, and many international student events are also being held here.

Cost: Entrance costs about $5 -- $10 for male and female customers. The drinks are very expensive so make sure to have the cash before going to this place.

Location: It is located in Wenceslas Square, and has a huge sign of the bar. The main club is at the rooftop of the building.

6. Radost FX

Radost FX is a small club in Prague, and its customers are mostly Americans. It became quite famous when Shakira shot her music video entitled Please Don't Stop the Music. Aside from being a nightclub, it's also a great vegetarian restaurant, and a famous breakfast place. If you get wasted after clubbing at night, you can kick – off your hangover in the morning by having their awesome European and American classic breakfasts.

Radost in Czech means joyful, and people who regularly come in this humble club can attest to that. Its interior has black and white couches, side bars as well as

Chapter Nine: Nightlife in Prague

back rooms where you can rest after dancing. Thursday nights is when the place popularly comes alive!

Cost: Also cost about $5 for male customers, women are free of charge. Drinks are relatively cheap than most bars and clubs in the city

Location: Belehradska 120, 12000 Praha (you can hop off the I.P. Pavlova metro station, it's just located across the tram stop)

Chapter Nine: Nightlife in Prague

7. *Estate House*

If you are not fond of clubbing or hanging out in bars, why not watch a classic opera at night? It can't get more European and classier than that! Witness the best operatic plays, and grand musical performances that Prague has to offer. You can also watch Prague's pride called Don Giovanni created by Wolfgang Mozart. It tells a story

Chapter Nine: Nightlife in Prague

about a womanizer who loves to play with women's feelings and eventually ends up in hell. This famous opera is constantly being played at the Estates Theater, where Mozart himself conducted his operatic music and plays many years ago.

    If you're not a fan of operas, you can still come here at night to gaze at the marvelous interior of the theater, and feel its overall ambiance that takes pride in many of the greatest musicians and art geniuses that played here.

Location: Ovocný trh, Prague 1

Website: www.ticketsonline.cz/tickets.php

Chapter Nine: Nightlife in Prague

8. *The Meet Factory*

Another interesting place you can go into at night is called the Meet Factory. Located in Smichov district, its exterior will be hard to miss because the building resembles a red car with two – fire engines made of fiberglass. It was a former factory converted into an art gallery, theater, music and film venue as well as a live entertainment facility. The building was created by David Cerny who is known as Prague's most controversial artist because his other works include men pissing off in front of the Kafka Museum, and giant babies crawling in telecommunication towers.

Chapter Nine: Nightlife in Prague

Local and international artist as well as tourists who are fans of art loves to come here to share the same passion and love for artistic works. The factory invites people all over the world to create and contribute different works of art. Perhaps, the most interesting and simplest but profound art work contributed is a wall inscription that reads: "Dear person who don't know me it's OK you don't know me. Best – A" (the author's initial).

Location: Ke Sklárně 3213/15, Praha 5-Smíchov, Czech
Tel. Number: +420 251 551 796
Website: www.meetfactory.cz/en

Chapter Nine: Nightlife in Prague

9. Reduta Jazz Club

For those who love to jam with jazz style of music then this is the club for you! Club Reduta had been around ever since Prague was under the communist control. It was popular back then until today. Around 1994, former president of the Czech Republic Vaclav Havel gave former U.S. President Bill Clinton a saxophone, Clinton then entertained the public with it.

Club Reduta is the go – to place for Blues, modern jazz, and Dixieland music among many. You can see many jazz posters on the venue's walls, and there are no waiters as well. You just have to serve yourself up with a drink you

Chapter Nine: Nightlife in Prague

like and enjoy the great jazz vibe around. Every night the club features different jazz musicians from around town. You should definitely go to this place if you want to feel the Dixieland vibe at night with family and friends.

Location: Národní 116/20, 110 00 Nové Město, Czechia
Tel. Number: +420 224 933 487
Website: www.redutajazzclub.com

10. Bar and Books

If you're a bit of nerd, a pretty square person, an introvert or someone who is looking for an interesting place to have a romantic yet interesting treat then Bar and Books is suited for you! The place is quite cozy, and great for meeting up with your cool and smart friends. The walls are painted in red, the furniture is made out of leather, and of course the bar has full of books! Or perhaps, it's a library that happens to have a bar inside it? Nevertheless, you will surely enjoy the calm oasis, and the classy vibe of the place while enjoying some drinks. You can chill with your girlfriends with a complementary cigar every Monday night because it

Chapter Nine: Nightlife in Prague

is Ladies' Cigar Night while Tuesdays are whiskey nights for both ladies and gentlemen.

You can enjoy different blends of cocktails like the popular Dark and Stormy as well as old time classic tonic and gins. You can also puff a cigar that originated from Cuba, Trinidad, and Dominican Republic. Another classic to try is their club sandwich paired with Russian vodka while watching a James Bond film! It's truly a classy night to remember!

Location: It is located in the Old Town Square, right at the center of Prague

Website: www.barandbooks.cz

Chapter Nine: Nightlife in Prague

Chapter Ten: Off - Beaten Path in Prague

Going off the beaten path in Prague is a must – try so that you can experience seeing the hidden facets of the city. It's a great way to discover many uncharted territories behind its already glorious façade. It's medieval atmosphere, friendly locals, and authentic European vibe will surely make you come back for more! So if you're a real backpacker, adventurer, and traveller then here are the ten best off - the - beaten paths you should take so you can look at the City of Golden Spires from a different perspective.

Chapter Ten: Off the Beaten Path in Prague

1. Kolbenka Flea Market

The Kolbenka Flea Market is tucked away in the neighborhoods of Kolbenova located in Praha 9 or district 9 of the city – center. You can easily get there without any hassle since Prague's transport system is accessible and efficient. Why not drop by on the weekends to shop around one of the largest flea market in the world! Just like in the medieval times, flea markets are the go – to place for everything food! You can find all the fresh ingredients, veggies and crops as well as fruits right out of the locals' farms.

Chapter Ten: Off the Beaten Path in Prague

You can also sell whatever you want since it is a flea market, the busiest days starts from Friday midnight until the weekends. You might want to go there early to find a good parking space if you have a car, but if you're going to hop on a train from the city – center, it will only take you about 15 minutes to reach Kolbenova where the Kolbenka Flea Market is located.

2. *Holesovice Neighborhood*

If you are a huge foodie, then the Holesovice neighborhood in Praha 7 will surely give you and your taste buds a run for your money! The former industrial spot just

Chapter Ten: Off the Beaten Path in Prague

right across the Vltava River is now buzzing with many cheap and local restaurants that serve breakfast, lunch, and afternoon snacks. You can head on over to Holesovice on the weekends with your family for a sumptuous local meal or spend your afternoon sipping coffee while hanging out with the locals.

Some of the best dining places and coffee houses includes Twenty7 Restaurant (mostly specializes in breakfast and lunch meals ranging from Mexican cuisine, European cuisine, and Asian cuisine), and Bitcoin Coffee among many. Bitcoin coffee is a coffee shop dedicated in using the crypto currency called Bitcoins or a virtual currency. If you're not tech savvy, don't worry because you can still pay in cash.

Chapter Ten: Off the Beaten Path in Prague

3. *Naplavka River Walk*

Another surefire off the beaten path that most tourists overlook is a walk by the Naplavka River. The second most scenic river in Prague (especially at night) is just located at the southern part of the Prague Castle. Aside from the magnificent view, you can also stroll around the vibrant riverside and check – out many restaurants, bars, and local music houses. The best time to walk around the Naplavka River is during summer, spring, and autumn season. On the weekends (Saturday morning until two in the afternoon), the

Chapter Ten: Off the Beaten Path in Prague

riverside also becomes a busy marketplace where most local farmers sell their fresh crops, vegetables, and fruits.

4. Jewish Cemeteries

If you're the morbid type, a history buff, or a proud member of the Jewish community, why not visit one of the most historical cemeteries in the country? The Jewish Cemetery located in Josefov deep inside the Jewish quarter dates back many centuries ago, and is one of the oldest Jewish cemeteries in Europe. It is where the most historical and famous people in the Czech Republic and Europe are buried. You can also find the best many ancient Jewish

Chapter Ten: Off the Beaten Path in Prague

synagogues around the area. In fact, many archaeologists cannot confirm how many bodies are buried ever since the cemetery was excavated.

You can also check out another nearby historical cemetery near Vysehrad Castle where most of the country's scholars and artists including Antonin Dvorak, and Mucha among many rests.

5. *Zizkov*

Zizkov is a residential place located at the hilltop of Vinohrady. Its unique building and housing structure is a must – see if you visit the area. There are no identical red

Chapter Ten: Off the Beaten Path in Prague

roofs, and the façades of each apartment are also different and unique.

Aside from a labyrinth of apartments and residential area, Zizkov is also home to the best bars in Prague. Bars are clustered here than in any other towns or districts of Prague. Many locals and tourist love to come here because of its various bar options. Here's a bit of trivia for you, Czech Republic is one of the top consumer of beers in the whole world! And Zizkov is the place where you can find the tastiest and most localized beer that Prague and the Czech Republic can offer!

Famous bars like Bukowskis, and Malkovich offers not just great liquors and spirits but also an enticing ambiance, and fine dining! If you like Charles Bukowski, the Bukowskis resto – bar will give you that century – old atmosphere paired with classy cocktails, and their best seller – the Naked Lunch! If you're looking for elegant drinks, you should try their reasonably priced beers, spirits, wines and cocktails. The restaurant's cozy setting is ideal for those who wanted to have an intimate dining experience.

Aside from Bukowskis, and Malkovich, you will find many interesting bars in Zizkov that you'll never find in any other countries! There are rock climbing bars, bowling bars and the likes. Many tourists overlook this area because it is

Chapter Ten: Off the Beaten Path in Prague

outside the city – center, but this off – the – beaten place will surely be worth visiting with your friends and loved ones.

6. *The Nový Svět*

The Nový Svět area was a former poor neighborhood in Prague. It doesn't have grand structures like in other towns but this neighborhood has unique charm to it because of its cobblestoned streets, unique houses, street lamps, and various art galleries. This long alley located just after the famous Prague Castle has a serene atmosphere that most tourists don't notice because they are being lured by the

Chapter Ten: Off the Beaten Path in Prague

grandiose architecture of other tourist spots nearby. If you continue to walk down past some residential areas, you'll eventually reach lesser known Baroque churches at Loreta's district. Wandering around the Nový Svět street is one of the greatest things you can do in the city – center without the hustle and bustle of tourists in nearby attractions.

7. Sea World

The Sea World Museum is a great place to visit especially for those who have kids. You can tour the little ones for them to see live sharks, fishes, corals, plants and

Chapter Ten: Off the Beaten Path in Prague

other water creatures. This underwater world that holds over 100,000 liters of water is perfect as part of your family trip.

The most famous feature of Prague's Sea World is the Sand Shark which is considered as the world's most feared shark, it measures about 3.5 meters in length but does not seem scary if you see it behind the glass. You can also go to this place every Tuesday to witness how they feed the sharks. There are also aquariums and other small fishes for small children to see at the lower level.

8. *Mirror Maze*

Chapter Ten: Off the Beaten Path in Prague

The Mirror Maze is another educational venue that is perfect for young ones and young at heart! It is located inside a mini castle in Petrin Hill; you can ride a cable car to get to the top of the hill easily. The building where the Mirror Maze is housed was part of the 1819 exhibition in Prague where various art forms like the miniature Eiffel Tower erected on top of the Petrin Hill was presented.

The cool thing about the Mirror Maze is that even though it looks like a tricky labyrinth, you will not lose your way but adult supervision is needed for very young children. Moms, dads and adults alike will surely have fun with a room full of distorting mirrors.

Chapter Ten: Off the Beaten Path in Prague

9. *Golden Lane*

The Golden Lane runs along the walls of the famous Prague Castle. The alley which was originally built for castle guards are now the hub and residential place of Czech's local artists, sculptors, and even goldsmiths.

If you stroll up to the far end of the Golden Lane, you'll eventually reach the Dalibor Tower where you will see a display of the instruments use for torturing people back then. You can then continue climbing up to see a sculpture called the Parable with the Skull, this modern

Chapter Ten: Off the Beaten Path in Prague

bronze work of art depicts a man with a very big skull in its back.

The Golden Lane's beautiful painted cottages are a perfect photo – op with your loved ones or friends. You can also avail a tour once you purchased a Prague Castle Complex Tour ticket.

10. Olomouc

Olomouc is located just outside the city – center. There aren't that much tourists around, which is ideal if you want to see the day to day lives of the locals. You can visit many places such as the bone church, castles, Palacky

Chapter Ten: Off the Beaten Path in Prague

University (Czech Republic's prestigious and one of the most populated universities in Europe), beautiful fountains, various local restaurants, and boutiques, St. Wenceslas Cathedral as well as a version of an astronomical clock inspired during the communist era.

You can also find a UNESCO World Heritage Site in Olomouc which is a gigantic plague column.

Chapter Ten: Off the Beaten Path in Prague

Quick Travel Guide

The Golden City of a Hundred Spires is something to be thankful for because despite of its long history and crazy turnovers from one ruler to another, its people still managed to keep its origins and historical essence that made it a great city intact. Although most countries and cities are progressively turning into a more modern and technology driven world, the city of Prague somehow embrace the future without letting go of its glorious past. Before this comes to an end, this chapter will provide you a quick travel guide that you can easily browse wherever you are. Šťastná cesta! (Happy trip!)

Prague Highlights

1. Prague Quick Facts

a. **Currency** – Czech Crown or koruna; (CZK or Kč)

b. **Primary Language spoken:** Czech, Slavic, Croatian, Polish, Serbian, Bosnian, Slovak, English

c. **Temperatures and seasons:**

- **Spring:** between March until May; this is a great time for tourists to explore this vibrant city because the weather is not too hot or too cold plus places aren't packed with tourists unlike during summer time

- **Summer:** between June to August; summer in Prague is the time where most tourists from all over the world and from neighboring European countries arrived. Expect crowds of visitors everywhere from cafes, dining places to tourist attractions and hotels. .

- **Autumn:** usually between September to October. Temperature ranges from 40 – 60 degrees Celsius so be sure to wear a couple of layers. Its major advantage is that there aren't many tourists compared to previous months, and the weather is also good.

- **Winter:** between November to February. The temperature can drop to 20 degrees and has an average high of about 30 degrees Celsius. You can expect almost no tourists at all! You can pretty much enjoy the city, feel it has a cool breeze, and also get cheaper accommodations

2. *Transportation*

Transportation Services in Prague

- Airplane
- Train/ Metro Stations (Domestic and International)
- Tram Stations
- Buses (Main City, Airport Transfers and some Remote Places)
- Taxis
- Bike Rentals
- River Cruise
- Car Rentals

3. Travel Essentials

Immigration and Visas

- If you are a tourist, you need to have a passport with 6 months of validity. A Schengen Visa may be required in some countries not included in the list (see list in Chapter 2). You can check out the consular website of the Czech Republic for more info.
- If you are planning to stay longer in Prague or the Czech Republic for an extended vacation or other private matters, you may need to show proof that you have sufficient funds that will last you for your intended period. You may also be asked to show a confirmed onward and return flight tickets, and also the address of the place you're going to stay in/ hotel booking confirmation.
- European Union citizens, family members of EU citizens, or family members of EU politicians/ government may not be required to have a Schengen Visa but some rules apply.

Money Exchange

- Czech Republic's currency is called Czech Crown (or koruna). The local abbreviation of the currency is Kč, while the international abbreviation is CZK.

- Exchange counters and offices in Prague offer very bad rates plus they also charge other fees. Make sure to ask the employee/s first on how much you would get if you exchange a certain amount before giving them your money so you can compare rates with other offices.

ATMs and Credit Cards

- ATMs are found almost everywhere and are available 24/7 but high charges may apply
- Credit cards such as American Express, Visa and MasterCard may be accepted in various hotels, restaurants, and shops but always make sure to bring cash on hand because most establishments don't accept cards.

Electric and Voltage

- Prague's standard electrical voltage is 220 – 240 volts AC (50 cycles).
- Majority of the plugs and electric outlets are European standard electrical sockets called the Type C Europlug as well as Type E, and Type F Schuko.

- Buy the three common kinds of adaptors to make sure that you can charge while in Prague.

Communication Services

- Telephone booths still exist in the city but they are only a few and may not be accessible. Most phones require a prepaid calling card that you can purchase from magazine kiosks or tobacco booths.
- You can choose to buy a pay – as – you – go SIM card plus a prepaid calling card in town. You may also opt to open your roaming services, although the charges will be a bit expensive (overseas charges) if you send international SMS or calls. UK cellphones may work without any problem as long as you activate international roaming features.
- The Wi-Fi and internet services in Prague are not that accessible. If you will be staying at hotels, they may also charge you for it, and the signal may drop if you're far from their routers. Don't expect any internet connections in remote areas.
- Internet cafes, some hotels, and business centers also offering internet access but you may need to pay for it to rent the computers.

Prague Highlights

1.) Where to Stay

Here's a quick list of the districts in Prague where you can stay during your trip.

- Praha 1 (The Old Town, The New Town, The Little Town/Castle Town)
- Praha 2 (Vinohrady and Namesti Miru)
- Praha 3 (Jiriho Podebrad Metro along the border of Vinohradska)
- Praha 4 (Branik and Podoli area)
- Praha 5 (Mala Strana River to the Zbraslav)
- Praha 6 (West and North of Castle Town to the boundaries of Prague 7 - Dejvice area)
- Praha 7 (Liben and Holesovice extending from the Letna River)
- Praha 8 (Karlin and Kobylisy)
- Praha 9 (Ceskomoravska area)
- Praha 10 (borders with Pragues 2, 3, and 9; eastern side of the Stredocesky district)

2.) Where to Eat

Here's a quick list of top restaurants you need to try in Prague.

- Aromi
- Bellevue
- *Blatouch*
- *Café Imperial*
- *Café Savoy*
- Cukrkvalimonda
- Hergetova - Cihelna
- Jahma
- Klub - Architekt
- U-Modr-Kachniky

3.) Tourists Spots

Here's a quick list of the famous tourist destinations in Prague:

- Charles Bridge
- Old Town Square
- Prague Castle

- Dancing House
- Estates Theater
- The Powder Gate
- Municipal House
- The Astronomical Clock and Old Town Hall Tower
- Wenceslas Square
- Vltava River

4.) Churches in Prague

Here's a quick list of the churches and synagogues you can visit while in Prague:

- Tyn Church
- *St. Vitus Cathedral (Katedrála svatého Víta)*
- St. Nicholas Church of Old Town Square
- Strahov Monastery (Strahovské nádvoří)
- St. Peter and Paul Church
- St. George's Basilica at Prague Castle (Bazilika Sv. Jiří)
- Spanish Synagogue
- Old New Synagogue

- The Church of Our Lady Victorious
- St. Salvator Church

5.) Museums in Prague

Here's a quick list of the famous museums you can go to while you are in Prague.

- *National Museum (Narodni Muzeum)*
- Dvorak Museum
- St. Vitus Cathedral Museum
- Prague Castle Museum
- Charles Bridge Museum
- The Museum of Communism
- *Mirror Maze Museum*
- Golden Lane
- Sea World Museum
- *Mucha Museum*

6.) Nightlife in Prague

Here's a quick list of the places you can hang out at night in Prague:

- *Club Sasazu*
- The Retro Club
- *Karlovy Lázně*
- Lucerna
- Duplex
- Radost FX
- *Estate House*
- The Meet Factory
- Reduta Jazz Club
- Bar and Books

7.) Off – Beaten Path in Prague

Here's a quick list of the unchartered territories you can explore in Prague.

- Kolbenka Flea Market
- Holesovice Neighborhood
- Naplavka River Walk

- Jewish Cemeteries
- Zizkov
- The Nový Svět
- Sea World
- Mirror Maze
- Golden Lane
- Olomouc

PHOTO REFERENCES

Page 1 Photo by user tpsdave via Pixabay.com, https://pixabay.com/en/prague-czech-republic-city-urban-1882884/

Page 5 Photo by user Pexels via Pixabay.com, https://pixabay.com/en/architecture-bridge-1845560/

Page 14 Photo by user kirkandmimi via Pixabay.com, https://pixabay.com/en/prague-flag-view-castle-sky-czech-1786448/

Page 18 Photo by user Terminals & Gates Flickr.com, https://www.flickr.com/photos/terminals/13361563673/

Page 19 Photo by user J Aaron Farr Flickr.com, https://www.flickr.com/photos/jaaronfarr/519948326/in/photolist

Page 39 Photo by user kirkandmimi via Pixabay.com, https://pixabay.com/en/prague-river-boats-sky-paddleboat-1912710/

Page 53 Photo by user kirkandmimi via Pixabay.com, https://pixabay.com/en/prague-city-modern-bridge-cars-2211919/

Page 55 Photo by user nike159 via Pixabay.com, https://pixabay.com/en/czech-republic-prague-old-town-2042799/

Page 58 Photo by user Megan Eaves via Flickr.com, https://www.flickr.com/photos/megoizzy/6932903524/

Page 60 Photo by user Monudet via Flickr.com, https://www.flickr.com/photos/monudet/4545973847/

Page 62 Photo by user Martin Hapl via Flickr.com, https://www.flickr.com/photos/haplm/4662046/

Page 64 Photo by user Donald Judge via Flickr.com, https://www.flickr.com/photos/donaldjudge/14426187611/

Page 66 Photo by user Leon Barnard via Flickr.com, https://www.flickr.com/photos/leonland/3997952200/

Page 68 Photo by user damian entwistle via Flickr.com, https://www.flickr.com/photos/damiavos/8381576178/

Page 70 Photo by user Pepik Hipik via Flickr.com, https://www.flickr.com/photos/pepikhipik/26055769181/

Page 72 Photo by user Felix Meyer via Flickr.com, https://www.flickr.com/photos/meyerfelix/8046366365/

Page 74 Photo by user Kurtis Garbutt via Flickr.com, https://www.flickr.com/photos/kjgarbutt/5496292175/

Page 77 Photo by user Anguskirk via Flickr.com,
https://www.flickr.com/photos/anguskirk/14534153059/

Page 78 Photo via Aromi Restaurant Official Gallery,
https://aromi.lacollezione.cz/files/aromi-new-4.jpg

Page 80 Photo via Bellevue Restaurant Official Gallery,
http://www.bellevuerestaurant.cz/gallery-en.htm

Page 82 Photo via Blatouch Official Gallery,
http://blatouch.cz/#fotogalerie

Page 83 Photo by user Dave Ungar via Flickr.com,
https://www.flickr.com/photos/ungard/6051283436/

Page 85 Photo by user Kent Wang via Flickr.com,
https://www.flickr.com/photos/kentwang/3023043001/

Page 87 Photo via Cukrkvalimonda Official Website,
http://cukrkavalimonada.com/

Page 89 Photo by user Roman Boed via Flickr.com,
https://www.flickr.com/photos/romanboed/15604919190/

Page 91 Photo by user Tom Hodgkinson via Flickr.com,
https://www.flickr.com/photos/hodgers/43565198/

Page 92 Photo by user solidarity via Flickr.com,
https://www.flickr.com/photos/i35south/3435076698/

Page 94 Photo by user Norio Nakayama via Flickr.com, https://www.flickr.com/photos/norio-nakayama/32636950686/

Page 97 Photo by user kirkandmimi via Pixabay.com, https://pixabay.com/en/prague-view-skyline-roofs-church-1903605/

Page 98 Photo by user peto23 via Pixabay.com, https://pixabay.com/en/prague-charles-bridge-vltava-1350542/

Page 100 Photo by user PublicDomainPictures via Pixabay.com, https://pixabay.com/en/architecture-bohemia-building-20923/

Page 102 Photo by user Coffee-King via Pixabay.com, https://pixabay.com/en/prague-castle-czech-historic-1788343/

Page 104 Photo by user LenaSevcikova via Pixabay.com, https://pixabay.com/en/building-the-dancing-house-prague-922531/

Page 106 Photo by user Jessica Gardner via Flickr.com, https://www.flickr.com/photos/pjgardner/1018187324/

Page 108 Photo by user Johnny Peacock via Flickr.com, https://www.flickr.com/photos/traverseearth/6780999224/

Page 110 Photo by user leiris202 via Flickr.com, https://www.flickr.com/photos/60584010@N00/22413665148/

Page 112 Photo by user Anguskirk via Flickr.com, https://www.flickr.com/photos/anguskirk/15680058175/

Page 114 Photo by user Miroslav Petrasko via Flickr.com, https://www.flickr.com/photos/theodevil/4419965131/

Page 116 Photo by user Dennis Jarvis via Flickr.com, https://www.flickr.com/photos/archer10/32176079044/

Page 119 Photo by user kirkandmimi via Pixabay.com, https://pixabay.com/en/religion-church-cathedral-vitus-2244034/

Page 120 Photo by user Nan Palmero via Flickr.com, https://www.flickr.com/photos/nanpalmero/34801181930/

Page 122 Photo by user Miroslav Petrasko via Flickr.com, https://www.flickr.com/photos/theodevil/7293432872/

Page 124 Photo by user Tony Hisgett via Flickr.com, https://www.flickr.com/photos/hisgett/2541116858/

Page 126 Photo by user Mphotographe via Flickr.com, https://www.flickr.com/photos/photos_mp/7864556420/

Page 128 Photo by user Al Case via Flickr.com, https://www.flickr.com/photos/60035031@N06/32668525231/

Page 130 Photo by user Dennis Jarvis via Flickr.com, https://www.flickr.com/photos/archer10/33020214885/

Page 132 Photo by user Mike Steele via Flickr.com, https://www.flickr.com/photos/21022123@N04/34919080841/

Page 134 Photo by user greynforty via Flickr.com, https://www.flickr.com/photos/greynforty/4447692727/

Page 136 Photo by user Em and Ernie via Flickr.com, https://www.flickr.com/photos/emandernie/6350881054/

Page 140 Photo by user Anguskirk via Flickr.com, https://www.flickr.com/photos/anguskirk/16245052084/

Page 141 Photo by user Ed Webster via Flickr.com, https://www.flickr.com/photos/ed_webster/14831356576/

Page 142 Photo by user Miroslav Petrasko via Flickr.com, https://www.flickr.com/photos/theodevil/4295168469/

Page 144 Photo by user Karen Blakeman via Flickr.com, https://www.flickr.com/photos/rbainfo/5824125188/

Page 145 Photo by user Tony Evans via Flickr.com, https://www.flickr.com/photos/tonyevans/26779607325/

Page 147 Photo by user Sue Manus via Flickr.com, https://www.flickr.com/photos/suespix/4954785347/

Page 149 Photo by user Miroslav Petrasko via Flickr.com, https://www.flickr.com/photos/theodevil/6955347806/

Page 151 Photo by user Mike Steele via Flickr.com, https://www.flickr.com/photos/21022123@N04/34982080212/

Page 152 Photo by user William Murphy via Flickr.com, https://www.flickr.com/photos/infomatique/32553754933/

Page 153 Photo by user Mikey V via Flickr.com, https://www.flickr.com/photos/mikey_loves_bcn/3993910185/

Page 154 Photo by user Mohylek via Flickr.com, https://commons.wikimedia.org/wiki/File:Lindley.jpg

Page 157 Photo by user Mister No via Wikimedia Commons, https://commons.wikimedia.org/wiki/File:Mucha_Museum_-_panoramio.jpg

Page 158 Photo by user Max Dawncat via Flickr.com, https://www.flickr.com/photos/maxdawncat/32747221896/

Page 160 Photo via Sasazu Restaurant Official Gallery https://www.sasazu.com/en/gallery

Page 162 Photo by Julien via Flickr.com, https://www.flickr.com/photos/djou/499166774/

Page 164 Photo by user Ulf Liljankoski via Flickr.com, https://www.flickr.com/photos/whyld/6083157012/

Page 168 Photo by user Paul van Dijk via Flickr.com, https://www.flickr.com/photos/paulvandijk/3419120731/

Page 170 Photo by user Sarah via Flickr.com, https://www.flickr.com/photos/srebouh/9013393813/

Page 172 Photo via Radost FX Official Gallery
https://www.radostfx.cz/en/club/photos/detail/interior

Page 174 Photo by user majorbonnet via Flickr.com,
https://www.flickr.com/photos/majorbonnet/136617253/

Page 176 Photo via the Meet Factory Official Website
http://www.meetfactory.cz/en/about

Page 178 Photo by user Joao M. Nogueira via Flickr.com,
https://www.flickr.com/photos/jnogueira/7599607340/

Page 179 Photo by user Sebastian via Flickr.com,
https://www.flickr.com/photos/bastispicks/3509236881/

Page 180 Photo by user Roman Boed via Flickr.com,
https://www.flickr.com/photos/romanboed/26585399972/

Page 182 Photo by user Jim Killock via Flickr.com,
https://www.flickr.com/photos/jimkillock/9641306437/

Page 183 Photo by user Tjflex2 via Flickr.com,
https://www.flickr.com/photos/tjflex/2844956030/

Page 184 Photo by user Chris via Flickr.com,
https://www.flickr.com/photos/eisenbahner/9658135470/

Page 186 Photo by user Al Case via Flickr.com,
https://www.flickr.com/photos/60035031@N06/34147625752/

Page 187 Photo by user jaime.silva via Flickr.com,
https://www.flickr.com/photos/20792787@N00/3356311266/

Page 189 Photo by user Mike Steele via Flickr.com, https://www.flickr.com/photos/21022123@N04/35139300035/

Page 190 Photo by user adrigu via Flickr.com, https://www.flickr.com/photos/97793800@N00/3680526584/

Page 191 Photo by user PavelH via Pixabay.com, https://pixabay.com/en/prague-prague-castle-czech-republic-961961/

REFERENCES

"10 Things to Do in Prague at Night" OverseasAttractions.com

<https://www.overseasattractions.com/inspirational/cities/10-things-to-do-in-prague-at-night/>

"10 Top Tourist Attractions in Prague" – Touropia.com

<http://www.touropia.com/tourist-attractions-in-prague/>

"Best Prague Restaurants" – 10best.com

<http://www.10best.com/destinations/czech-republic/prague/restaurants/>

"Best Times to Visit Prague" - U.S. News Travel Guide

<http://travel.usnews.com/Prague_Czech_Republic/When_To_Visit/>

"Churches" – Prague – Guide.co.uk

<http://www.prague-guide.co.uk/category/churches/>

"Culture of Prague" – Yatra.com

<https://www.yatra.com/international-tourism/prague/culture>

"Entry Requirements & Customs" – Frommers.com

<http://www.frommers.com/destinations/prague/planning-a-trip/entry-requirements--customs>

"Getting Around" – Frommers.com

<http://www.frommers.com/destinations/prague/planning-a-trip/getting-around>

"Getting Off the Beaten Path in Prague" – JustAPack.com

<https://www.justapack.com/off-the-beaten-path-prague/>

"Getting There" – Frommers.com

<http://www.frommers.com/destinations/prague/planning-a-trip/getting-there>

"Health & Insurance"– Frommers.com

<http://www.frommers.com/destinations/prague/planning-a-trip/health--insurance>

"History of Prague through the Centuries" – My Czech Republic

<http://www.myczechrepublic.com/prague/history/prague_history.html>

"Nightclubs in Prague" - LikeALocalGuide

<https://www.likealocalguide.com/prague/nightclubs>

"Off the Beaten Path in Prague: 5 Suggestions" - ThisIsMyHappiness.com

<http://thisismyhappiness.com/2013/01/18/off-the-beaten-path-in-prague/>

"Prague: 10 Things to Do" – Time.com

<http://content.time.com/time/travel/cityguide/article/0,31489,1925095_1921770_1921733,00.html>

"Prague" – CzechTourism.com

<http://www.czechtourism.com/a/prague/>

"Prague" – Wikipedia.com

<https://en.wikipedia.org/wiki/Prague>

"Prague" – Wikitravel.com

<http://wikitravel.org/en/Prague>

"Prague History Facts and Timeline" - World – Guides.com

<http://www.world-guides.com/europe/czech-republic/prague/prague_history.html>

"Prague: Bars, Pubs & Clubs" – InYourPocket.com

<https://www.inyourpocket.com/prague/nightlife>

"Prague Jewish Town" – CzechTourism.com

<http://www.czechtourism.com/c/prague-jewish-town-synagogues/>

"Prague Money" - Frommers.com

<http://www.frommers.com/destinations/prague/planning-a-trip/money>

"Prague Sights & Attractions" – PragueExperience.com

<https://www.pragueexperience.com/sightseeing/highlights/museums-art-galleries.asp>

"Staying Connected" – Frommers.com

<http://www.frommers.com/destinations/prague/planning-a-trip/staying-connected>

"The Best Areas to Stay in Prague" – LivingPrague.com

<https://livingprague.com/prague-accommodation/where-stay-prague/>

"The 10 Best Prague Hotels" – TripAdvisor.com

<https://www.tripadvisor.com.ph/Hotels-g274707-Prague_Bohemia-Hotels.html>

"Top 10 Off the Beaten Path Places in Prague" – Untapped Cities

<http://untappedcities.com/2015/03/06/top-10-off-the-beaten-path-places-in-prague/>

"The 10 Most Beautiful Churches in Prague" – The Culture Trip

<https://theculturetrip.com/europe/czech-republic/articles/the-10-most-beautiful-churches-in-prague/>

"The Best Museums to Visit in Prague" – The CultureTrip

<https://theculturetrip.com/europe/czech-republic/articles/the-best-museums-to-visit-in-prague/>

"Things to do in Prague – 50 Best Places to Visit!" – TravelTipy.com

<http://www.traveltipy.com/most-beautiful-places-in-prague-and-around/>

"Visa Information for tourists visiting Prague" – Prague Experience

<https://www.pragueexperience.com/information/visas-passports.asp>

"Where to stay in Prague: Best Areas & Hotel" – Touropia.com

<http://www.touropia.com/where-to-stay-in-prague-best-areas-hotels/>

"Where to Stay in Prague: Prague Neighborhood Guide" – Wandertooth.com

<https://www.wandertooth.com/where-to-stay-in-prague-neighbourhoods/>

Feeding Baby
Cynthia Cherry
978-1941070000

Axolotl
Lolly Brown
978-0989658430

Dysautonomia, POTS Syndrome
Frederick Earlstein
978-0989658485

Degenerative Disc Disease Explained
Frederick Earlstein
978-0989658485

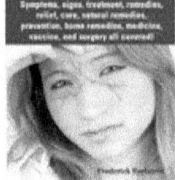

Sinusitis, Hay Fever,
Allergic Rhinitis Explained
Frederick Earlstein
978-1941070024

Wicca
Riley Star
978-1941070130

Zombie Apocalypse
Rex Cutty
978-1941070154

Capybara
Lolly Brown
978-1941070062

Eels As Pets
Lolly Brown
978-1941070167

Scabies and Lice Explained
Frederick Earlstein
978-1941070017

Saltwater Fish As Pets
Lolly Brown
978-0989658461

Torticollis Explained
Frederick Earlstein
978-1941070055

Kennel Cough
Lolly Brown
978-0989658409

Physiotherapist, Physical Therapist
Christopher Wright
978-0989658492

Rats, Mice, and Dormice As Pets
Lolly Brown
978-1941070079

Wallaby and Wallaroo Care
Lolly Brown
978-1941070031

Bodybuilding Supplements
Explained
Jon Shelton
978-1941070239

Demonology
Riley Star
978-19401070314

Pigeon Racing
Lolly Brown
978-1941070307

Dwarf Hamster
Lolly Brown
978-1941070390

Cryptozoology
Rex Cutty
978-1941070406

Eye Strain
Frederick Earlstein
978-1941070369

Inez The Miniature Elephant
Asher Ray
978-1941070353

Vampire Apocalypse
Rex Cutty
978-1941070321

www.ingramcontent.com/pod-product-compliance
Lightning Source LLC
Chambersburg PA
CBHW071700090426
42738CB00009B/1597